The Professional Studio Vocalist

Claytoven Richardson

THOMSON

COURSE TECHNOLOGY

Professional ■ Technical ■ Reference

Some of the definitions in this book are reprinted with permission from *The Dictionary of Music Business Terms* by Tim Whitsett, Mix Books, 1998.

Photos by Phil Bray Photography, Oakland, CA; Jackie West Photography, Oakland, CA; Dan Schmalle, Chris Konovaliv, and Paul Stubblebine, San Francisco, CA; Daniel Norton, New York, NY; Mackie®; and Roland Corp®.

Doonesbury comic strip provided by G. B. Trudeau, copyright 1986. Reprinted with permission of Universal Press Syndicate. All rights reserved.

Web Site Content: Audio files recorded at Subway Studios, Oakland, CA. Voiceover Talent: Isaac Stevenson "Vocal Cords In Action" video provided by Pacific Voice and Speech Foundation.

Thomson Course Technology PTR and the author have attempted throughout this book to distinguish proprietary trademarks from descriptive terms by following the capitalization style used by the manufacturer. All trademarks are the property of their respective owners.

Educational facilities, companies, and organizations interested in multiple copies or licensing of this book should contact the Publisher for quantity discount information. Training manuals, CD-ROMs, and portions of this book are also available individually or can be tailored for specific needs.

ISBN-10: 1-59863-279-5
ISBN-13: 978-1-59863-279-8
Library of Congress Catalog Card Number: 2006923479
Printed in the United States of America
07 08 09 10 11 TW 10 9 8 7 6 5 4 3 2 1

Publisher and General Manager, Thomson Course Technology PTR:
Stacy L. Hiquet

Associate Director of Marketing:
Sarah O'Donnell

Manager of Editorial Services:
Heather Talbot

Marketing Manager:
Mark Hughes

Marketing Coordinator:
Adena Flitt

Executive Editor:
Mike Lawson

Project Editor:
Dan Foster, Scribe Tribe

PTR Editorial Services Coordinator:
Erin Johnson

Interior Layout:
Shawn Morningstar

Cover Photo:
Phil Bray Photography

Cover Designer:
Elizabeth Paquin

Indexer:
Sharon Hilgenberg

Proofreader:
Megan Wade

Artwork:
Claytoven Richardson

Model:
Sandy Griffith

Transcriptionist:
Yvonne Bennett

Author Biography:
Hillel Risner

THOMSON

★

COURSE TECHNOLOGY™

Professional ■ Technical ■ Reference

Thomson Course Technology PTR, a division of Thomson Learning Inc.
25 Thomson Place ■ Boston, MA 02210 ■ http://www.courseptr.com

Acknowledgments

Creating this book has been about a 5-year process, and through it all there have been some very instrumental people in my life whom I cannot thank enough. I want to express my heartfelt appreciation to:

First and foremost, God for being the guiding light in my life.

Mike Lawson, for your belief in me, and for facilitating this opportunity for me to share my knowledge with others.

Stacy Hiquet, Dan Foster, Mark Hughes, Beth Paquin, and all of the other wonderful people at Thomson Course Technology for turning my voice into ink for all to see.

It is said that a man is nothing without his family, and I have some gems more precious than the most flawless of diamonds in my wife, Catheryn, and my daughters, Ashley and Cameryn. You are my world. Thank you for putting up with me during this entire process.

My best friends, Larry Batiste, Michael Denten, and Dooney Jones, and their families for being some of my biggest supporters throughout the years.

Susan McLean, for being the spark that got me so interested in the business of being a professional studio vocalist.

The staff, past and present, at the AFTRA/SAG and Recording Academy (NARAS) offices in San Francisco, California.

Evelyn Miller-Mack, Joy Thompson, Craig Abaya, Jon Bendich, Michael Aczon, and all the rest of the staff, instructors, and students of the Music Recording Industry department at San Francisco State University.

The many teachers, producers, engineers, record exec's, managers, booking agents, musicians, and vocalists with whom I have worked and who have become my friends and extended family. It would take me a lifetime to name you all.

The Harris/Overstreet family for welcoming me into your family with open arms—and especially to Nana Zella, the best mother-in-law in the world.

There are two people to whom I must give my greatest thanks: my parents Phebia Richardson and the late David Richardson. Thanks for my brothers (David, Jr.; Brian; and Philip) and their families, and my sister (Michelle) and her family. I love them all very much. Mom and Dad, your endless sacrifices have helped me to realize many of my goals and dreams. You are my inspiration. I hope one day when I grow up that I can be just like you.

About the Author

Serendipity gave **Claytoven Richardson** both his name and a jump-start to a career as a top session singer. But his good fortune had started years earlier, in the form of music education.

Although he grew up in a tough East Oakland, California, neighborhood, Richardson's shaping forces were positive. Instead of hanging out on the streets in high school, Richardson toured Europe with one of the premier choirs of that time, Phil Reeder's Castlemont High chorus, The Castleers. "While in that group, it was my first time leaving the country and learning that the world was bigger than my little neighborhood," says Richardson. Instead of getting into trouble in high school, he studied clarinet and saxophone at the San Francisco Conservatory of Music and entered UC Berkeley's Young Musicians Program (YMP) for gifted, "at-risk" youngsters. YMP instructor Bill Bell became "like my second father," says Richardson. "He'd teach me arranging, how to score compositions. I learned music just from basically being part of his family."

Thanks to those instructors and many others, Richardson went to the University of Michigan on a full scholarship as an oboe principle. It was during one of his school vacations that he acquired a name that neatly described the direction his life was taking. Childhood friend (and now business partner) Larry Batiste accidentally fused Richardson's given name, Clayton, with that of another artist, and out came "Claytoven." The impressive name stuck, and its owner determined to work hard to live up to it.

Claytoven's singing career was also unintentional. After college, he played sax with and co-produced Bill Summers and Summers Heat. Summers overheard Claytoven singing reference vocals to get the sense of a song and then asked Claytoven to perform lead. He has been in demand as a session singer ever since, singing background vocals on countless gold and platinum recordings featuring Kenny G, Tevin Campbell, Michael Bolton, Elton John, Peabo Bryson, New Kids on the Block, Ricky Martin, Whitney Houston, Mariah Carey, Jennifer Lopez, Aretha Franklin, Natalie Cole, and many others. His work on the number-one song for Celine Dion, "My Heart Will Go On" (also the title track for the *Titanic* soundtrack), won him Grammy recognition in 1999.

In addition to his many other accolades, Claytoven was presented the "Key to Creativity" award by the City of Oakland in recognition of his outstanding achievements in the performing arts. "This was truly the greatest honor that I have ever received. It is so wonderful to be thought of like this at home."

In 1994, Claytoven started Claytoven Music Entertainment (CME) to facilitate managing all of his music business endeavors, some of which include music production, CD artwork designs, and Web site designs. CME also co-manages a production studio in Oakland where Claytoven devotes himself to writing catchy, contemporary compositions, which have been recorded by Lisa Fischer, Shanice Wilson, Al Jarreau, and Patti Austin, among others.

But as busy as he is, Claytoven always makes time for educating others. "I was blessed as a kid," Claytoven says. "Because of the many teachers who came into my life while still in high school, I got to talk with Duke Ellington and ask questions about his music. I got to play with Max Roach and Abbey Lincoln. I feel it is my responsibility to pass on my knowledge to young musicians just as it was passed on to me." And with that as his mission, Claytoven has stepped into the role of instructor at San Francisco State University (SFSU). There he teaches two professional music classes for SFSU's Music Recording Industry department ("The Role of the Record Producer" and "Studio Training Workshop for Vocalists"). "With music education in public schools dwindling, it becomes that much more important for professional musicians to educate the young music community."

Contents

Chapter 4
Getting Studio Work   39

Chapter 5
Taking Care of Business   49

Chapter 6
The Hiring Call   67

Chapter 7
Professionalism   71

Chapter 8
Studio Boot Camp   83

Chapter 9
Lead Vocals   111

Chapter 10
Background Vocals

131

Chapter 11
Thoughts from a Few Professionals

145

Epilogue

173

Appendix

175

Glossary

193

Index

207

Preface

It was around 1994, and my career was really beginning to take off as a background vocalist when a good friend of mine, Susan McLean, asked me if I wanted to serve as a board member for AFTRA (American Federation of Television and Radio Artists). She worked for the San Francisco chapter of this union at the time and thought it would be a good idea for at least one singer to be on the board to represent the needs of singers in the Bay Area. She felt it was especially important because at that time the board consisted of only radio and television announcers. Apparently, she did a good job of convincing me because there I was running to become an AFTRA board member. To my surprise, the members of the chapter voted me in.

There I was in the thick of some very important decision-making, like artists' rights and fair treatment of singers by producers and record companies. The experience helped me to become well versed in the ways of the union as well as the music business at large. The board worked hard at helping the Bay Area vocalists to convince producers, production companies, and record companies to do more of their projects through the union, and the board also helped them understand why it was so beneficial for them to do so. But as I saw these wonderful changes transpire, I also noticed that although the producers, production companies, and record companies were steadily advancing in knowledge and expertise in dealing with professional studio vocalists, many of the Bay Area singers were not as versed about their own profession.

There were a lot of places for people to learn how to become a good singer, but there was nowhere for them to learn how to become a professional singer, especially with regards to being in a professional studio setting. Well, that sparked a fire in me. During my next recording sessions, I started notating exactly what I and the other singers in the recording sessions did. The realization quickly came to me how studio singers took for granted much of what was really done in a recording session. So I spent the next couple of years researching, gathering, and organizing my notes. In the year 2000, those annotations spawned into my first university course, "Studio Training Workshop for Vocalists." The goal of the workshop was to help bridge the gap between the academic and professional music worlds by providing aspiring singers and producers with hands-on experience in a professional recording studio environment. Students were guided through myriad subjects, including recording studio basics, professionalism, union basics, taking care of business, as well as vocal techniques for both lead and background studio singing. Students also learned techniques on proper headphone use, how to blend with others, choosing the right microphone, protocol for session singers, guidance toward finding employment as a session singer, and much more. This comprehensive workshop covered the basic training necessary to pursue a career as a professional studio vocalist. I brought in industry professionals like Patti Austin, Philip Ingram, Tony Lindsay, and others as guest speakers. I sponsored the class solely until 2005 when I formed an alliance with San Francisco State University's (SFSU) Music Recording Industry department.

I still teach my workshop at SFSU; however, through my many travels recording in different cities throughout the United States, I soon realized that this information is needed in more than just the Bay Area. And that brings me to the purpose of this book. Though I can't give you actual in-studio experience, I can impart to you a plethora of information and techniques important for garnering and maintaining a career as a professional studio vocalist. Also, through the magic of today's technology, I can give you exercises via this book's companion Web site (www.courseptr.com/downloads). It is my hope that you will take full advantage of the years' worth of experience put into this book and use it to help reach your goals and dreams.

How to Use This Book

Through my work as an educator and vocalist I have encountered a great many aspiring singers. Time after time, when talking with them these same questions seem to pop up consistently:

* How do I become a studio singer?

* What must I do in preparation for that career?

* What should I know before I go into my first recording session?

Well, this book provides straightforward answers to those questions as well as easy-to-follow explanations of more of the most important issues involved in becoming a professional studio vocalist. You will find that this book is geared toward the beginner to intermediate singer. If you are a bit more advanced, not to worry; you will still find a lot of information from which you will benefit greatly.

The chapters are set up to somewhat mimic the process that a vocalist would go through while developing a studio singing career. The structure of this book is what I call an accumulative process. It is much like the way math is taught. You start out with the basics of addition and subtraction and then you progress into multiplication and division. Soon you are up to algebra, geometry, and calculus, with each progressive step requiring the previous as its foundation. You couldn't work with the Pythagorean theorem or with word problems without first understanding all of the concepts at their foundations. So I encourage you to go through this book in a chronological manner. If you find that a particular chapter covers something that you already know, then by all means skip ahead.

DEFINITIONS

I could never stand it when books required me to jump back and forth to a glossary whenever I encountered any new terminology. So, in addition to including a glossary at the end of this book, I will spare you the annoyance of constantly turning pages back and forth by also including definitions within the text.

 Next to this icon you'll find definitions of important words.

There will be a lot of terminology and basic technical knowledge that you will need to thoroughly understand, so please take the time to look at those definitions. Some of the definitions will be a bit narrow in scope, but that is only because my goal is for you to understand the terminology from the perspective of a vocalist, not a recording engineer.

SPECIAL NOTES

Throughout this book, there are concepts that need more clarification than is appropriate within the text. There are also additional instructions that I'll give. Please take note of these comments or instructions whenever you see the icon below.

 Next to this icon will be special comments or instructions.

WHAT'S ON THE COMPANION WEB SITE?

Additional materials and updates to this book are available on the companion Web site. Simply go to **www.courseptr.com/downloads,** where you will find audio and video examples of vocal techniques and exercises for you to practice as well as other useful reference materials. When discussed in the book, you'll see a reference number next to the text that will enable you to easily find the corresponding item on the companion Web site. See the Appendix for a list of the Web site content.

You are also invited to visit my Web site, www.claytoven.com/educational. Check out "The Student Lounge" by clicking on its link and typing the password "practice." This Web page contains items such as other recommended books, songwriter and singer contests, auditions, activities, events, and other interesting information.

If you have any questions about any of the information contained in this book, you're welcome to e-mail me at info@claytoven.com.

How Skilled Are You?

I made my start as a clarinetist and saxophonist. Throughout my childhood, my parents sent me to every music camp or school they could find. Later, I went to college and played woodwinds, with my principal instrument being the oboe. My chosen major was music education at the University of Michigan. As an instrumentalist, my life was totally and wonderfully inundated with music.

Lead Vocal/Lead Vocalist/Lead Singer: To be the featured singer.

Background Singer/Background Vocalist: A vocalist who backs up a featured vocalist or instrumentalist with harmonies, responses, and choruses.

Vibrato: A pulsating effect produced in a vocal tone by barely perceptible, minute, and rapid variations in pitch.

Blend: A balance of volume and timbre within a group of vocalists.

Fate is such as strange thing; through a twist of fate I went from being an instrumentalist to a vocalist almost overnight. Being a vocalist so far has been a great ride. I especially like not having to carry around heavy instruments anymore. (I can almost see the cringing instrumentalists who don't like hearing that.) Early on, I realized that since I was on the path of being a singer that maybe I should take some singing lessons to gain some control over my voice. Through my experiences as an instrumentalist, I had things like proper breathing techniques, music reading, and other basic music skills fairly mastered, but I found that private vocal lessons really helped. A lack of vocal control certainly will show when you're singing *lead vocals*, but nowhere near as much as when you're a *background singer*. For background singing, it becomes very important to know how to change the speed of your *vibrato* or how to sing without vibrato. You must also know how to control your voice enough to *blend* with other singers. (Further discussion on blend will follow later.)

BASIC MUSICIANSHIP

When I started singing on *commercial sessions* and movie soundtracks I quickly found that all of the training I had received as an instrumentalist was not in vain. After so many sessions of learning the vocal parts by ear, all of a sudden I was handed music *charts*. My knowledge of how to read music enabled me to gain and keep more of those types of *gigs*. The point is that my education and experience in the basic music disciplines has helped me attain the levels of success that I have enjoyed over the years. So although this book will impart a lot of professional information and techniques, remember that there is no substitute for basic musicianship. If you haven't done so already, I seriously encourage you to take classes in one or more of the following musical disciplines:

*   **Basic Music Theory/Fundamentals of Music.** These skills include basics such as note recognition, clefs, rhythmic notation, etc. and are very helpful if you want to be able to read and write music.

*   **Sight Singing and Ear Training.** Sight-reading music, understanding the relationships between notes (intervals), as well as auditory recognition of intervals and chords are definitely needed skills if your goal is to have any kind of sustained career as a professional vocalist.

✳ **Private Vocal Lessons.** Learning and strengthening basic singing skills and techniques is very important for learning how to use and care for your voice properly.

Maybe you feel that taking a class in music theory or sight singing might be a bit overwhelming right now. Or perhaps you don't consider taking these classes because they are not offered at a school nearby. Well, thanks to the wonders of the digital world, there are computer programs that can help. Consult with your local music store or, better yet, do an online search. Just go to one of the Internet search engines like yahoo.com or google.com and type into the search field the phrases "music theory" and "software." You should be able to find a software program that will suit your needs.

Commercial: An advertisement aired on television or radio.

Session/Recording Session: A period of time scheduled for recording music or vocals.

Chart: A written arrangement or part for musical instruments or vocalists.

Gig: A job, especially a booking for musicians.

Musicianship: The art of being skilled in music.

Following is a brief "General Knowledge Quiz," the answers to which can be found at the end of this chapter. Yeah, yeah, just what you needed, another test. This quiz, however, was designed to help you get a gauge on where you are with regards to your musical and technical knowledge. If you do not want to write in your book, a .pdf version of the "General Knowledge Quiz" (ws_02-01.pdf) can be found on this book's companion Web site, www.courseptr.com/downloads.

General Knowledge Quiz

1. The vocalist on the session is singing "P's" too hard, causing a pop sound. What device will help with this problem?

    a. Gobo

    b. wind screen

    c. baffle

2. A *cardioid* pattern is best described by which shape?

    a. circle

    b. heart

    c. figure eight

3. One of the vocalists on a session took off his headphones too close to the live microphone, causing what sound?

    a. sweetening

    b. bleed

    c. feedback

4. Singing below the proper or indicated pitch is

    a. flat

    b. harmony

    c. sharp

5. What type of microphone is most often used to record vocals in the studio?

    a. ribbon

    b. condenser

    c. dynamic

6. If an engineer tells you that a microphone is hot, he is saying

    a. that it is off

    b. that it is on

    c. that it is overheating

7. One of the vocalists on a session asked for a lyric sheet. Why?

    a. it contains the melody to the song

    b. it contains the chords to the song

    c. it contains the words to the song

8. The producer wants you to sing the vocal part without the music. He is asking you to sing

    a. flat

    b. *a cappella*

    c. cold

9. In common time, what note gets half of a beat?

    a. eighth note

    b. quarter note

    c. half note

10. Four people singing in a group is commonly known as a

    a. sextet

    b. quartet

    c. trio

11. A period of time scheduled for a specific purpose, such as a music recording, is called a

    a. session

    b. appointment

    c. planner

12. What is this "♩" symbol?

    a. quarter note

    b. whole note

    c. half note

13. When recording vocals, a pre-amp is typically used to

    a. run speakers

    b. power a microphone

    c. power headphones

14. A triad is

    a. three people singing together

    b. a three-song CD

    c. a three-note chord

15. What device can imitate the sound of you singing in an auditorium?

    a. compressor

    b. digital delay

    c. reverb

16. What note is a fifth above C?

    a. F

    b. D#

    c. G

17. If you pan a sound full left, in what approximate position would the pan pot be?

    a. 12 o'clock

    b. 7 o'clock

    c. 5 o'clock

18. What term is used to describe the music background for commercial advertisements?

    a. bed

    b. side

    c. sweetening

19. The producer has asked you to sing the minor third in a Bb minor chord. What note would you sing?

    a. F

    b. Gb

    c. Db

20. *Ritard* means

    a. a slow speed

    b. to slow down

    c. to reduce your vibrato speed

ANSWERS, EVALUATION, AND RECOMMENDATIONS

Answers to the "General Knowledge Quiz"

1.b, **2.**b, **3.**c, **4.**a, **5.**b, **6.**b, **7.**c., **8.**b, **9.**a, **10.**b, **11.**a, **12.**a, **13.**b, **14.**c, **15.**c, **16.**c, **17.**b, **18.**a, **19.**c, **20.**b

If you found that you had a hard time with the technical questions (1–3, 5–6, 11, 13, 15, and 17–18), not to worry: all of this will be covered later in the book. But these questions do give you a small idea of what's to follow. If you had a hard time with the musical questions (4, 7–10, 12, 14, 16, and 19–20), then please consider my earlier recommendation: seek out an appropriate class or course of study.

Many of these musical terms and concepts, and much more, will appear throughout this book. To get the most out of all the information contained in this book, you really should make sure that you have a good handle on basic musicianship.

Promoting Yourself

The hardest part to getting your career going is figuring out how to let the right people know that you exist, and that you have something special to offer. In the beginning, you will be your best salesperson. But like any good salesperson, you need a plan and the right set of tools. In this chapter, you will learn what goes into creating that plan and the tools that are required before putting that plan into action. I'll start off with some basics.

WHAT IS PROMOTION?

Promotion is the planning and execution of any and all activities necessary to sell your services, or as singers laughingly say in the entertainment industry, "...to get your hustle on." The first thing to delve into regarding self-promotion is planning. Most people have no problem with the execution aspect of things, though at times that execution is rather aimless. Sometimes there are people who are fortunate enough to fall into a career that way; however, for the majority of us it is important to remember that "if you fail to plan, then plan to fail." Now, I can't help you with the exact detailing of your plans simply because your end goals and circumstances may be different from that of other readers of this book. However, I can tell you that for every set of plans you will need information and tools to accomplish the goals set out in those plans. Let me help start your planning process by giving you tips on information you will first need to gather.

✳ **What are your services?** Take some time to figure out your singing strengths: the styles of music you can sing, whether you are good at reading charts, whether you have a great ear for harmony, and any other skills that you might have as a vocalist.

✳ **Why will people hire you?** Equally as important as the "what" is to figure out the "why factor." Why are your services special? What skills can you offer that others cannot? Do you have a singing style that is both broadly appealing and original?

✳ **What work experiences and educational background do you have?** Make a list of all the professional experience you have. List all industry-related education. Compile any news articles or reviews, video clips, audio clips, and existing demos.

✳ **What are your goals?** What do you want to accomplish as a singer (e.g., touring with a band, being a recording artist, working as a studio singer, becoming an actor)? Where do you want your singing career to take you (e.g., fame, living comfortably, fulfilling a dream)?

✳ **Who uses your services?** Start doing research on who hires people with your skills. Find out the types of projects for which they hire and how to contact them. A good place to start is the library, where there are tons of reference books with contact information for producers, managers, commercial production companies, *advertising agencies*, and more. Don't be afraid to do searches on the Internet for information. Just about anything you need to know can be found in a book or somewhere on the Internet. Check out the credits printed in audio CD booklets of the CDs that represent the styles of music that you like to sing. Call some of the many *trade organizations* like the National Academy of Recording Arts & Sciences (NARAS; a.k.a., The Recording Academy) or the National Association of Recording Industry Professionals (NARIP). (See the appendix for a long list of trade organizations and what they do.) Also, do research on networking opportunities like *trade shows*, conferences, and seminars.

Advertising Agency: A business that provides the service of producing advertisements for commercial products or services.

Trade Organization: An association of people engaged in a particular area of business organized for a specific purpose.

Trade Show: A large gathering of manufacturers of a particular classification of products.

Once you have gathered all of this information, it is time to move on to the next step: putting together a set of good promotional tools.

PROMOTIONAL TOOLS

In most instances a potential client's first impression of you will be made via some type of promotional item: a business card, a Web site, a photo, or a demo. That first impression, of course, should be a great one. You always want to put your best foot forward. So put some time and effort into your promotional tools. I know, you're thinking, "Man, this could cost me some serious bucks." Well, that's not necessarily true, but if you have to spend a bit more money than you want, isn't your career worth it? Let's talk about some of the promotional tools that you will need, and I'll give you some ideas on getting them made without possibly sacrificing an arm and a leg.

Business Cards

If you're planning on doing any professional business, you will need business cards. This is one of the most basic tools used to distribute your contact information. In most situations, exchanging business cards will be part of your initial contact with a potential client. Whether or not you have a business card plays a major role in that person seeing you as a professional and could also mean the difference between you getting the gig or not. How the card looks plays a role as well. So when it comes to putting your business cards together, do not skimp. Your business card should be unique and creative (see Figure 3.1). You want it to be something that will be a reminder to the recipient of your personality (see Figure 3.2). You also want your card to stand out from other business cards. And let's not forget, the card has to be informational too. Make sure that you include what you do and the ways that you prefer to be contacted. By the way, if you have a Web site and/or an e-mail address, definitely include that information.

Figure 3.1

Here's a clever use of the singer's silhouette to create a business card that is memorable.

Figure 3.2

The caricature on this business card gives a glimpse into this singer's personality.

There are several routes you can take to get your business cards done, some of which include the following.

DIY. If you own or have access to a computer and a printer with sufficiently high resolution, you can print your own business cards. There are several word-processing, graphic design, and label-making programs that have templates for designing and printing your own business cards. This is probably the cheapest way to go, but you should go this route only if you have stellar graphic artist skills. Owning one of these programs does not necessarily make you a graphic artist.

 Business card templates done in a couple of the more popular programs can be found on the companion Web site (ws_03-01.doc, ws_03-02.pm65, and ws_03-03.ai).

Web Sites. There are several Web sites that specialize in providing low-cost business cards. The price range that I've seen starts from $6 for 250 full-color cards created from a set of template designs that the company has available, to $70 or more for 1,000 full-color cards created from an initial graphic design that you submit. If you go the latter route, you will have to factor in the cost of having a graphic artist design the cards, which could be from $10 to $200 or more depending on how elaborate of a design you want.

Duplication Services. Most copy centers offer business card printing as a part of their services. It is usually outsourced to a third party, but the work is ordered through the copy center. The cost of 1,000 business cards can start at around $40 for a simple, one-color *thermograph* printed card with a graphic design that you provide. Thermograph cards are great if your design consists of mostly text. *Logo* artwork will sometimes work, as long as it is not overly detailed. Again, you will have to factor in graphic design costs, although some copy centers also have graphic design services available to help with designing your business card. These services are an extra cost, but probably not as much as it would cost if you hired an independent graphic artist.

Offset Printers. For more high-end cards, you can go the offset printing route. The cost could start at $75 or more for 1,000 cards, and, again, you will have to factor in the cost of having a graphic artist design the cards.

Thermograph Printing: Also called thermography or raised-ink lettering. This printing process creates a raised image on things like business cards, letterhead, or envelopes.

Logo: A symbol or other small design used by an organization or person to identify its products or services.

Biography

A biography, or "bio" as it is sometimes called, is your opportunity to talk about your background and skills. So take full advantage. Your bio should highlight your professional experience as a performer. If you are a newcomer with very little or no experience, your bio should comment on your educational background. Your bio could also talk about some of the things that you may have done vocally in high school or college. Your goals and where you see your career in the future should be mentioned. Some of the better biographies that I have read have a story—something that keeps the reader's interest. Remember that people who read your bio won't know you, so you want the facts about your career to be delivered in a way that won't bore them to death.

If you're writing your bio yourself, don't forget to write it in the third person. If it is done in the first person, you run the risk of appearing as if you are a braggart. A bio works a lot better when it takes on the tone of someone from the outside tooting your horn. If you don't quite have the writing skills to put together your bio, find someone you are certain can do the job effectively.

Whether you or someone else writes it, the goal again is to try to make your bio as interesting as you possibly can. But here's a caveat: by all means tell the truth. Do not use any unwarranted name-dropping that could have you looking embarrassed later. The circle of people in the music business is fairly small; potential clients receiving your bio will most likely check up on the facts surrounding name-dropping. You don't want to be caught trying to explain "inaccurate" or "exaggerated" information.

> *"Make your bio as interesting as possible, but by all means tell the truth."*

Keep your bio to one page. Especially in the beginning of your career, few people will have the time or desire to read your lengthy bio. You should have a condensed version that is no more than half a page long, as well as a one-paragraph version and a one-sentence version.

If you have a lot of recording experience, consider, in addition to your bio, putting together a *discography* (an abbreviated version of my discography is in the Appendix).

 Discography: A comprehensive list of the recordings made by a particular performer.

Photography

The most common promotional photo size is 8 inches by 10 inches. Over the years, that photo size has become the industry standard— so much so that promotional photos are often referred to as "8 by 10" (see Figure 3.3). These promo photos are used in a variety of ways: for news articles, for sending to potential clients, for Web sites, for promoting gigs, and much more. So it is important to have great photos. However, along with the increased accessibility of today's digital cameras, there now exists a greatly increased possibility of committing a serious *faux pas*: Unless you are willing to spend at least $700 or more for a professional-quality camera, today's digital cameras typically do not have the resolution required for taking the type of promotional shots you will need. That may change in the near future, but as of this writing, you should not try to use consumer model digital cameras. Because your photos will be scrutinized regularly, you should find a skilled photographer to take your pictures.

Laura Alhstrand

Figure 3.3

An example of an 8" x 10" headshot.

amazon.com

Billing Address:
ANNALISE OPHELIAN
465 DUBOCE AVENUE
SAN FRANCISCO CA 94117
United States

Shipping Address:
Annalise Ophelian c/o Morgana
740A 14th Street #199
San Francisco CA 94114
United States

SDYbv27syR

Returns Are Easy!
Visit http://www.amazon.com/returns to return any item -including gifts- in unopened or original
condition within 30 days for a full refund (other restrictions apply).

Your order of June 10, 2010 (Order ID: 105 – 6560970 – 2344245)

Qty	Item		Item Price	Total
	IN THIS SHIPMENT			
1	The Professional Studio Vocalist (Book) (** P-2-B37A144 **) 1598632795 1598632795 1598632795 Paperback	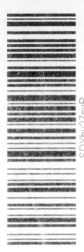	$29.99	$29.99

Subtotal		$29.99
Shipping & Handling		$3.99
Order Total		$33.98
Paid via Visa		$33.98
Balance Due		$0.00

This shipment completes your order.

Have feedback on how we packaged your order? Tell us at www.amazon.com/packaging

8424 (1 of 1)

SDYbv27syR

amazon.com
and you're done.™

1/DYbv27syR/-1 of 1-//CPSP/next/532737/0610-15.00/0610-13.25/sp0342184241/-1 1A3

Set up a photo shoot with a photographer who specializes in commercial or "acting" photography. Don't go to the local mall to get your glamour shots. Places like Wal-Mart or Sears can do great family and casual shots, but the type of photos you will need are quite different. Also, getting photos done that are really artistic is fine if you are putting together a CD to be released to the public for sale or if you are trying to get a record deal, but they do not lend themselves to what you need to get studio work.

Makeup Please

Once you've scheduled your photo shoot, you may want to consider hiring a makeup artist. I know that this is a sensitive subject for all of the manly men out there, but photos have a way of emphasizing things that sometimes aren't too flattering. If you have oily skin, the photo will make you look very shiny. If your skin is a tad uneven in tone, that will show up in the photo. A good makeup artist can make you look very natural while minimizing these types of problems. Also, if you have a flare for the dramatic, the makeup artist can help you create that look. Of course, as important as a great makeup artist can be to your photo shoot, there are always things that cannot be fixed no matter how much makeup is applied.

Make sure that you get plenty of sleep the day before your photo shoot. The last thing you want is to spend money on pictures in which you look sleepy or that feature the bags underneath your eyes. Try not to schedule the photo shoot for after school or work. Your tiredness will show up in the photos. If anything, take the day off and spend it preparing your clothes and getting your hair done for the photo shoot. No drinking of alcoholic beverages at least a day prior to the photo shoot; alcohol tends to make you look tired and also can give you red eyes. Do bring a bottle of Visine to the photo session—not to disguise red eyes from drinking alcohol, but to use for any other factors that may cause eye irritation such as smoke fumes, putting in contacts, recent swimming, or anything else. Red eyes will definitely show up in photos, even a black-and-white photo.

Making the Prints

Once you've had your photos taken, you will need prints. There are two conventional ways for making the prints.

* **Regular photo printing,** as done at most photo centers. There are also companies that specialize in printing larger quantities of photos. As already stated, most prints that you will need will be 8 by 10s. You'll also need to choose the type of finish: matte or glossy. Glossy is the best choice for all-around use. Matte-finished photos are a bit harder to scan properly, which is what most newspapers or magazines do if they want to use a photo for a printed article.

* **Lithograph printing.** A bit more cost effective are lithograph prints that are printed on heavy, satin-finish paper. The lithograph printing method produces an image that resembles a photograph so closely that most people cannot tell the difference.

Digital data files are a necessity and are something you should have in addition to prints created by one of the methods above. Be sure to ask the photographer to create a few high-resolution *JPEG* and/or *TIFF* files, and have him save them for you on a photo CD or on your hard drive or flash drive. These digital files will come in handy for uses such as within a Web site, e-mailing to clients, and a host of other graphic design purposes.

JPEG/JPG: Acronym for the *Joint Photographic Experts Group.* Pronounced *"jay-peg."* JPEG is a type of digital image used mainly on the Internet.

TIFF/TIF: Acronym for *tagged image file format,* one of the most widely supported file formats for storing digital images on personal computers.

The Demo

Some of the other names that you will commonly hear used for demos are *audition* reel, audition tape, demo reel, demo DVD, demo CD, and demo tape. The demo usually consists of audio and/or video of your performance and is prepared for the specific purpose of submission to record companies, commercial production companies, etc., so that your talent can be evaluated.

The Content of Your Demo

There are several different types of work you can get as a *studio* singer: commercial work, background vocals for record projects, movie sound track work, voiceover and singing work for game makers, *industrials*, and song demos for songwriters. Because there is a plethora of job types, even beyond those I have just mentioned, it is important for your demo to be specific to the type of job you are trying to get. If what you want is to work as a country background singer, you should do a demo singing country music. If you are trying to get into *jingles* or commercial work, *producers* generally will want to hear you in that type of setting. Put together demos for each type of job in which you would like to be involved.

 Throughout this book, the words *producer* and *client* will be used alternatively. However, note that although a producer can be the client, a client is not always the producer. For example, while working on a commercial session, the client could be an advertising agency that has hired a producer to oversee the recording process.

When putting together your demo, remember to keep it short and to the point. I recommend doing *snippets* of the best parts of songs rather than the full songs. A good length for a snippet is about one minute. As a general rule, keep the total length of your demo to no more than 5 to 10 minutes. Most people who listen to demos usually have tons of them to plow through and won't always have the time to listen to full songs or lengthy demos. Regardless of whether you do full-length songs or not, always put your best performance first. It could be that your potential client may only have time to listen to one song. You want that one song or snippet—that one *chance*—to be your best.

If your sole aspiration is to become a recording artist, then, short of having someone as your financial backer, you will need to put money together for a producer, a studio, and whatever other expenses may be involved. I recommend a great book that deals with many of the legal aspects of becoming and being a recording artist by a colleague of mine, Michael Aczon. The book is titled *The Professional Musician's Legal Companion* (see Figure 3.4) and is also published by Thomson Course Technology (www.courseptr.com). The road to becoming a recording artist is something I won't cover in this book; however, as you read on you

Figure 3.4

The Professional Musician's Legal Companion by Michael Aczon.

will find that part of the path is very similar to becoming a professional studio singer. You will also find that much of the information and techniques that I share will be of value if you are currently working toward a recording contract.

Audition: A tryout by a singer to demonstrate performing skills.

Studio: A specially designed, constructed, and equipped room or facility used for audio recording.

Industrial: Recording projects that are usually produced for large corporations or trade associations to introduce new products and sales promotions, etc.

Jingles: Short, catchy songs that are recorded and broadcast on TV or radio commercials.

Producer: A person or an organization that creates, or caused to be created, a product for sale; that organizes, guides, and shapes a product from conception to actuality.

Snippet: An abbreviated version of an audio file (song) or video.

The reality is that there are far more opportunities available in a career as a professional studio vocalist. If being a star is not your primary goal, then before you dig into your pockets and haphazardly hire a producer and schedule studio time, there are some music alternatives to consider. You can find a wealth of great *Karaoke tracks* online that you can use to help create your demo. Two wonderful former students of mine, Karen Smith and Reuben Confer, turned me on to a couple of really cool Web sites: pocketsongs.com and colonymusic.com. There are a few other useful Web sites, but the majority of my students seem to like those two the most. The great thing about doing your demo with Karaoke tracks (that is, if the tracks are recorded well) is that the listener can concentrate on how your voice sounds rather than being distracted by an original song that is unfamiliar.

Karaoke Tracks: Prerecorded backing tracks of popular songs that people can sing to.

Hire a Producer!

Even if your demo will consist only of Karaoke tracks, hire a producer. You really need someone who has experience in the studio. This person can help make the recording session a much smoother process. You definitely should consider hiring a producer if you are going to use musicians, engineers, or any other recording-related personnel. Your main concentration should be as a singer. Believe me, being a singer in the studio is a big enough task. Before you set out to find and hire a producer, however, it is important that you truly understand the producer's role in the recording process. So, let's review what a producer is and what a producer does.

"A producer is a person or an organization that creates, or causes to be created, a product for sale; that organizes, guides, and shapes a product from conception to actuality." From this definition, you can see that the producer has a big job. It also gives you an indication of some of the qualities that are important for the producer. A good producer:

* Has a thorough understanding of what a producer does
* Has the ability to handle a great deal of responsibility
* Has an excellent understanding of music
* Has very good multitasking skills
* Has the ability to work well with others
* Is a good organizer
* Has great listening skills
* Is very creative

Finding a Studio

Next you will need a studio in which to record. And believe me when I say that there are plenty of studios ready and waiting to take your money to help you put together a demo. The great news is that with today's affordable new music technology, there are lots of people making music in home studios; in small project studios; and in the larger, more traditional commercial studios. If you took my advice and hired a producer, your producer can probably recommend a couple of good studios. You can also ask other singers and musicians for referrals to good studios in which they have worked. Look for a studio that:

* Is a comfortable environment in which to work. Is the studio space too cramped or too cold? Is this the perfect place for you to sing your best? What attributes might make the studio convenient for everyone who needs to work on your project? (Is it easy to find? Does it have enough good parking, etc.)

* Has the proper recording equipment for your project. This especially includes a few good vocal microphones. (I'll talk about microphone choices a bit later.)

* Has accommodating studio hours. Maybe you can only work mornings or late nights.

* Has a great rate. Sometimes studios even offer what's called a "block rate" for recording time. You get a block amount of time for a set price, which is usually lower than the studio's regular hourly rate.

* Comes with a *recording engineer*. A recording engineer is usually offered as a part of most commercial studios' services. The recording engineer should possess some of the same qualities as I mentioned for a producer. Ask the studio owner or manager plenty of questions. If the recording engineer does not meet your qualifications, you will have to consider hiring an independent recording engineer; however, most large commercial studios usually have great recording engineers as a part of their draw. Note that I said, "*most large commercial studios...*"!

The majority of smaller project, home, and even some commercial studios may not have an engineer on staff. Many of the home and project studios may have the owner running the recording equipment. That could be a good or bad thing, depending on that person's experience and skills.

Again, a good producer can help you with figuring out your studio needs. Don't be afraid to shop around. With a little patience and perseverance, you should be able to find a great place to record your demo for a great price.

Recording Engineer: One who is trained or professionally engaged in capturing, maintaining, manipulating, and mixing audio performances.

Demo Alternatives

For yet another alternative, see if you can find up-and-coming songwriters or producers who need someone to sing on their demo projects. They might be willing to work a trade, with the benefit to you of getting a copy of the project to use as part of your own demo. Think creatively. What are some of the other tradable music and non-music skills that you may have to offer? Maybe you can trade some carpentry skills in return for one of your songs being produced. Anything and everything is negotiable.

"If you fail to plan, then plan to fail."

Quality

No matter what route you take to get your demo recorded, it is important that the resulting demo be done as professionally as possible.

The vast majority of potential clients are used to hearing professional-sounding CDs. Every once in a while you may run across a person who has the ability to distinguish between a good vocal and a bad demo, but sending a badly done demo on the hopes of running into one of those people is an awfully big chance to take. The safest bet is to compare your demo to what you hear on the radio or in your CD collection. Make sure that the lead vocal is featured prominently volume-wise and not buried underneath the music. Finally, if your demo doesn't stand up to other CDs that you listen to, you should consider re-recording the demo or even hiring another producer or recording engineer to help you get it right.

Video Demos

Another alternative to consider is that video demos are often acceptable. Understand, however, that there is a convenience factor to consider. DVD players are quite prevalent and affordable today, but VCRs aren't available as much anymore. Plus, DVDs can be played in most of today's computers. Still, the best thing to do is to ask clients whether they would prefer to receive a VHS tape, a DVD, or just an audio CD.

Some of the same ideas I provided for getting an audio demo done can also be applied to video demos. I won't get into a dissertation on video production since video demos are an option and not the current standard for getting studio work, but the main thing is to make sure that your video footage stands up to the following criteria:

* This is your best performance. If you can't honestly say that it is your best performance, do not use it.

* The picture quality is great. Make sure that there is no graininess in the picture quality. The picture should not be blurred and should have excellent brightness and contrast.

* It has good sound quality. Doesn't sound distorted; doesn't sound too roomy.

* The editing is smooth and professional looking.

* The video is packaged in a professional manner.

Your Demo Package

The presentation of your demo is something that you also have to consider. Let's say, for instance, that you go to a department store to buy a couple of pairs of pants and just happen by the CD section. You start to think about buying a couple of CDs of some artists that you have been hearing a lot about. You then pull three CDs from the bins. Two have pristine-looking artwork, while the third looks like it was printed very shoddily. You take a look in your pocket and realize that you have only enough money to buy two CDs. My question to you is: Which two will you most likely buy? My bet is that you will buy the two with the better visual presentation. Potential clients look at demo packages in much the same way. A shoddily done demo package could possibly wreck your chances of being heard. So put some time into the presentation of your CD just as you would for your business cards.

Following are some options for putting together the presentation of your CD or DVD:

 As I said before in the section on business cards, if you don't have stellar "Do-It-Yourself" graphic artist skills, then please "Do Yourself" a favor and hire a graphic artist. Enough said.

DIY. If you own or have access to a computer and a printer with sufficiently high resolution, you could print your own CD or DVD labels. Most word-processing, graphic design, and label making programs have templates for designing and printing labels. Some inkjet and laser jet printers will even print directly on CDs or DVDs that have printable white surfaces. Your computer will also need to have either a CD or a DVD burner and a burner program for you to make copies.

CD and DVD Manufacturers. These companies specialize in manufacturing high-quality CDs and DVDs. Printing is done directly on the CDs and DVDs using a silk-screening method, while the inserts and tray cards are usually done on offset printing presses. For this high-end printing process, be prepared to spend about $900 and up for CD manufacturing, and even more if you're having DVDs made. Also, because of the time required to set up the printing presses, most manufacturers often will not take print orders of less than 1,000 units. Even if they will print smaller amounts, it winds up being so expensive that you might as well have the 1,000 printed.

Many manufacturers have CD and DVD packaging design templates as well as design specifications available for download on their Web sites.

Short-Run Manufacturers. There are several CD manufacturers that can do what's called "short runs." Short runs are any amounts of printing less than the standard 1,000 units minimum. Instead of using the costly silk-screening and printing press methods, they use a high-end version of the DIY method. They can then produce short runs of high-quality CDs and DVDs at much more affordable prices.

CardDiscs. For all of you techies out there, here is my favorite. A CardDisc is a 3-inch disc that will play in just about any CD or DVD player with a tray drive. The front of the disc can contain all of the information that you would normally put on a business card. The discs also come in different shapes. Each disc can hold from $50MB$ to 175MB of data for CDs and 300MB to $1.2GB$ of data for DVDs, depending upon the shape you decide to use. That's more than enough space for a nice-length audio or video demo. They are rather expensive to have manufactured, but when you consider that you are getting two promotional items in one, the price may not seem so intense. I particularly like that when giving a potential client one of these CardDiscs, I have not only handed them my business card, but at the same time I have handed them my demo. Many CD and DVD manufacturers such as Acutrack (www.acutrack.com), Disc Makers (www.discmakers.com), and Kaba Audio (www.kabaaudio.com) have these multimedia discs available in different shapes. Consult with these and other companies that you can find on the Internet for the styles and shapes they have available.

Digital Copies

The digital world plays an integral part in the music industry nowadays, so you should definitely have high-resolution digital copies made of your audio demos in all of the following formats: *aiff, wav,* and *mp3.*

MB (megabyte): A unit of measurement of data capacity of computing items such as hard drives, CDs, DVDs, computer memory, etc. A megabyte is loosely equal to one million bytes, with a byte being one unit of memory size.

GB (gigabyte): A unit of measurement of data capacity of computing items such as hard drives, CDs, DVDs, computer memory, etc. A gigabyte is loosely equal to one billion bytes, with a byte being one unit of memory size.

Aiff/Aif: Acronym for *Audio Interchange File Format.* An audio file format standard used for storing sound data on personal computers. Originally developed for use on Apple computers.

Wav/Wave: Short for *Waveform* audio format. An audio file format standard used for storing sound data on personal computers. Originally developed for use on PCs.

mp3: *MPEG-1 Audio Layer 3* is a digital audio encoding and compression format designed to reduce the amount of data needed to represent audio.

Web Site

Nowadays having a Web site is just as important as having a business card, if not more important. It is the perfect billboard for showcasing all of the promotional materials that you've just read about.

Following are some of the design elements to consider when planning and constructing your Web site.

✳ **Who is your target audience?** Who you are aiming your Web site toward will make a big difference in figuring out the setup of the site. If you are trying to get a record deal, maybe the site should be a bit more artsy. If you are trying to get work, perhaps the site should be more businesslike in appearance.

✳ **What will visitors learn about you?** Is it that you want them to see how great of a vocalist you are in a particular field? Maybe you want them to understand how experienced you are via your biography or discography.

✳ **What hosting service will you use?** There has to be a place for your Web site to live that is accessible to the general public 24/7 via the Internet. There are Web site hosting companies such as RCN (www.rcn.com), Verio Network Services (www.verio.com), Host Baby (www.hostbaby.com), and Uniserve Online (www.uniserve.com) specializing in that service.

✳ **Do you have a *domain name*?** My domain name is "claytoven.com." If you want that kind of identifying address for your Web site, you will have to go to a domain name registration company to set that up. Two of the popular companies are Network Solutions (www.networksolutions.com) and Tucows (www.tucows.com).

✳ **What content do you want to include** (e.g., logo, biography, photos, audio, video, news clippings, etc.)?

✳ **Will you need a Web site designer?** I think this is worth saying one more time: You should go the route of DIY only if you have stellar graphic artist skills. Plus, someone who is skilled and experienced in Web design will give you ideas on content, a good hosting service, and more.

 Domain Name: A custom identifier for a Web site. (See the Glossary for a more in-depth explanation.)

A while back, I took a Web site design class at my local community college. I really wanted to learn as much as I could about all that it takes to put together a good Web site. Toward the end of the quarter, the instructor gave us all the assignment of finding a business or individual that needed a Web site and creating their Web site as our final projects. Some of the students did not have anyone that they could think of, and the instructor responded with a list of people who were interested in having a Web site done. Am I hearing bells, chimes, and gongs? The ideas must be flowing like crazy right now. One of the ways to get a Web site done, or at least started, could be via college students who need to design Web sites for their final class projects. Aren't you glad you thought of that?

If you must go the way of DIY, there are what are called WYSIWYG ("What you see is what you get"—pronounced, "wizzy wig") computer programs available. Two of the most popular programs are Adobe Dreamweaver and Microsoft Front Page. Thomson Course Technology has great instructional books on both programs, which you can find at www.course.com. You will still need to have some basic knowledge of HTML, JavaScript, and possibly CGI Scripts and CSS. If these acronyms kind of just went over your head, that's all the more reason to hire a Web site designer.

Another option available to you is via Web hosting companies that offer what they call Web site design wizards. You need no experience in HTML or any of the other Web design programming languages. You just go to the host's Web site and set up an account. Once your account is set up, you are then allowed to choose from a set of templates. The wizard (interactive Web pages set up to help you create your Web site) then guides you through the process of customizing your chosen template to fit your needs.

PUTTING TOGETHER A BUDGET

A major component of planning is preparing a budget. Before you start spending money haphazardly, you should put together a "Promotional Tools Budget." I've started one for you (see Figure 3.5). Pay close attention to all of the categories. Copy this example budget and add any new categories that are unique to your situation. Make calls to the appropriate people and companies to get accurate amounts to fill in. Do not factor into your budget favors or trades. I can't tell you how many times I've witnessed people factoring into a recording budget a guitarist coming in to play for free or a buddy coming to help out with some vocals, only to find out later, once they were already underway with the recording project, that the favor did not exist. All budgets from situations like these can result in the project being stalled for an indefinite period of time. If you do have access to a favor or a trade, deal with it later as a windfall. Keep the real prices in your budget and put money away for those items just in case. Once you have completed your budget, you will have a better idea of what you may have to spend or where you may have to make cuts. Also, this would be the perfect time to prioritize what you want to get done first based upon your financial abilities.

An Excel template of the Promotional Tools Budget can be found on the companion Web site. (ws_03-04.xls).

Promotional Tools Budget

Business Cards

Final # of Business Cards 1,000

	Names	Rate	Cost	Spent
Graphic Artist-Logo	Stanley Ashton Graphics	50.00	50.00	50.00
Graphic Artist-Layout	Stanley Ashton Graphics	35.00	35.00	35.00
Printing	Two Stars Printing	75.53	75.53	75.53
	Total Business Cards		$160.53	$160.53

Biography/Discography

Final # of Biographies 500

	Names	Rate	Cost	Spent
Writer	Art Sigerman	75.00	75.00	60.00
Graphic Artist	Stanley Ashton Graphics	25.00	25.00	25.00
Printing	Two Stars Printing	36.24	36.24	36.24
	Total Biography/Discography		$136.24	$121.24

Photography

Final # of Photo Prints 500

	Names	Rate	Cost	Spent
Photographer	Ted Dawson Photography	300.00	300.00	300.00
Makeup Artist	Shirley Laws	120.00	120.00	120.00
Printing	Thompson Lithography	76.36	76.36	76.36
Miscellaneous	Stellar Graphics (photo CD)	11.84	11.84	11.84
	Total Photography		$496.36	$496.36

Recording (The Demo)

Final # of Songs 3

Rehearsal

	Names	# of Days	Rate	Cost	Spent
Rehearsal Facility	Star Audio	1	90.00	90.00	75.00
Musicians	Alex Sams (Keyboard)	1	50.00	50.00	50.00
	Don Adams (Drums)	1	50.00	50.00	50.00
	Todd Gray (Guitar)	1	50.00	50.00	50.00
	Jan Thomas (Bass)	1	50.00	50.00	50.00
	Rehearsal Total			$290.00	$275.00

Personnel

	Names	# of Songs	Rate	Cost	Spent
Producer	Yon Dickerson	3	1,000.00	3,000.00	3,000.00
Production Assistant	(N/A)	0	0.00	0.00	0.00
	Producer (Sub-Total)			3,000.00	3,000.00

	Name	# of Hours	Rate	Cost	Spent
Engineer	Included in studio	0	0.00	0.00	0.00
	Engineers (Sub-Total)			0.00	0.00

	Names	# of Songs	Rate	Cost	Spent
Arranger	Sam Harrison	1	200.00	200.00	200.00
Copyist	Sandy Lee	3	55.00	165.00	165.00
	Arranger/Copyist (Sub-Total)			365.00	365.00

Figure 3.5

A sample budget. (The amounts in this sample are for example only and could vary greatly.)

Musicians

Names	# of Songs	Rate	Cost	Spent
Alex Sams	3	200.00	600.00	600.00
Don Adams	3	200.00	600.00	600.00
Todd Gray	3	200.00	600.00	600.00
Jan Thomas	3	200.00	600.00	600.00
	0	0.00	0.00	0.00
	0	0.00	0.00	0.00
Musicians (Sub-Total)			2,400.00	2,400.00

Musicians Payroll Costs

	Base Pay	Rate	Cost	Spent
Payroll Costs	2,400.00	2.5%	60.00	0.00
AFM EPW		10.0%	240.00	0.00
AFM H&W		23.0%	552.00	0.00
Payroll Taxes		16.0%	384.00	0.00
Musicians Payroll (Sub-Total)			1,236.00	0.00

Vocalists

Names	# of Songs	Rate	Cost	Spent
Allison Gray	2	200.00	400.00	400.00
Todd Gray	1	200.00	200.00	100.00
	0	0.00	0.00	0.00
	0	0.00	0.00	0.00
Vocalists (Sub-Total)			600.00	500.00

Vocalists Payroll Costs

	Base Pay	Rate	Cost	Spent
Payroll Costs	600.00	2.5%	15.00	0.00
AFTRA H&W		11.0%	66.00	0.00
Payroll Taxes		16.0%	96.00	0.00
Vocalists Payroll (Sub-Total)			177.00	0.00
Total Personnel			$7,778.00	$6,265.00

Studio Time

	Studios	# Of Hours	Rate	Cost	Spent
Recording	Inner Star Recording	6	65.00	390.00	390.00
Overdubs & Editing	Inner Star Recording	4	65.00	260.00	260.00
Mixing	Inner Star Recording	12	65.00	780.00	780.00
Other studio costs…		0	0.00	0.00	0.00
	Total Studio Time			$1,430.00	$1,430.00

Equipment and Instruments

	Items	Cost	Spent
Equipment Rental	Allantown Music - rented a Motif	100.00	100.00
Equipment Purchase		0.00	0.00
Instrument Rental		0.00	0.00
Instrument Purchase		0.00	0.00
Cartage		0.00	0.00
	Total Equip. & Instr.	$100.00	$100.00

Figure 3.5 (continued)

A sample budget. (The amounts in this sample are for example only and could vary greatly.)

Media Costs

	Items	Quantity	Unit Price	Cost	Spent
Hard Drive (bkup)	160gb Tandem Drive	1	159.67	159.67	129.32
DVDs (10 pk)		0	0.00	0.00	0.00
CDs (50 pk)		1	16.27	16.27	10.61
			Total Media Costs	$175.94	$139.93

Miscellaneous Expenses

	Items	Cost	Spent
Travel	Gas money for Allison & Todd Gray	30.00	30.00
Lodging		0.00	0.00
Food		0.00	0.00
Refreshments		0.00	0.00
Other...		0.00	0.00
	Total Misc. Expenses	$30.00	$30.00

Recording Total

	Cost	Spent
Rehearsal Total	290.00	275.00
Total Personnel	7,778.00	6,265.00
Total Studio Time	1,430.00	1,430.00
Total Equip. & Instr.	100.00	100.00
Total Media Costs	175.94	139.93
Total Misc. Expenses	30.00	30.00
	$9,803.94	$8,239.93

Demo Packaging - Manufacturing

Final # of Demo Packages   1,000

	Names	Rate	Cost	Spent
Graphic Artist	Stanley Ashton Graphics	500.00	500.00	500.00
Manufacturing	Carrier CD Manufacturing	1,173.32	1,173.32	1,173.32
		Total Manufacturing	$1,673.32	$1,673.32

Web Site

	Names	Rate	Cost	Spent
Web Site Designer	Stanley Ashton Graphics	400.00	400.00	300.00
Domain Name	IP International	0.00	0.00	0.00
Web Site Hosting		0.00	0.00	0.00
		Web Site Total	$400.00	$300.00

Budget Summary

	Cost	Spent
Business Cards	160.53	160.53
Biography/Discography	136.24	121.24
Photography	496.36	496.36
Recording (The Demo)	9,803.94	8,239.93
Demo Packaging - Manufacturing	1,673.32	1,673.32
Web Site	400.00	300.00
Budget Total	**$12,670.39**	**$10,991.38**

Figure 3.5 (continued)

A sample budget. (The amounts in this sample are for example only and could vary greatly.)

Getting Studio Work

Of course, all the information you need has been researched and gathered and all of your promotional tools are in place now, right? Without that preparation, this chapter would be like putting the cart before the horse, so I will assume that you have everything in order.

FIRST THE TRUTH (REALITY CHECK)

I want to talk about putting all of that information and those tools to work, but first I need to be perfectly honest with you. Reading this book does not guarantee that you will have a career as a professional studio vocalist, nor is there an easy way of getting studio work. There is definitely no single approach. Although, with that being said, the ability to be a little "nicely" aggressive is a big start. Don't be afraid to speak up for yourself and your skills when the occasion arises. My mother used to say, "A closed mouth never gets fed." Aside from a little "nice" aggressiveness, there are two major traits common in most successful studio vocalists: consistency and persistence.

Consistency is doing what you say you're going to do when you say you're going to do it, and being where you say you'll be when you say you're going to be there. Man! That was a mouth full. In the music business, a great deal of weight is placed on your word. Garnering a reputation of faulty reliability is a sure way to have a short-lived career. If you know that you can't do something or be somewhere at a proposed time, do not make that commitment.

Persistence is basically...keep trying, keep trying, keep trying! You'll need to learn to embrace the word "no" as if it were your best friend. You're going to hear that word in some form or another with regularity before you finally hear the magical word "yes." Rather than freaking out over a negative response to your demo or audition, try to remember that "no" is usually just another way of saying "You're not ready yet" or "You're not what we're looking for right now." Don't let "no" be a discouraging factor in your career. Keep forging ahead, and, at some point, usually when you least expect it, things will start to happen for you. Okay, enough with that pep speech.

GOALS AND DIRECTION

The beginning of Chapter 3 was the primer to figuring out your goals. It's time to get a bit deeper. I'm going to pose to you two questions again from that chapter and one new question. This time I want you to think very carefully about them. Then write down your answers in detail.

* What type of singer do you want to be?

* What do you want to accomplish as a singer?

* Where do you want your singing career to take you?

The answers now become the basis of your goals. Once you've set these goals, post them where you will see them regularly. Try to direct all of your everyday activities toward reaching your goals. If that means going back to school, then by all means enroll. If it means practicing an hour more each day, then do so. By the same token, if you find that you are doing things that don't fit in the scheme of your goals, it's time to make a change. Life throws all sorts of twists at you, but do your best not to be derailed. Do, however, keep your mind open. You never know where your success will come from. I started out as a clarinetist and became a vocalist. Who knew? Don't be afraid to modify your goals when you see fit. I am attaining the things that I want; I just had to realize that the path was going to be a bit different than what I had planned. Don't be afraid to take a detour, as long as you know you're headed in the right direction.

> *"A closed mouth never gets fed."*

You now have completed another part of your plan: solidifying your goals. What's next?

THE PROMOTION REALLY BEGINS

If you plan to get any work, you have to do three things:

* Inform people that you exist.
* Tell them why they should hire you.
* Convince them to hire you.

To accomplish this, you have to meet people. You will also need to develop and build a database (snail mail or e-mail), so it's time to throw yourself out there.

The hardest thing to becoming a studio vocalist is getting heard. You might think that it is as easy as making a demo of your best work and handing it to every potential client you know. Well, to a small extent that is true; however, if that person is getting demos from a host of other singers, why would that person want to put your demo at the top of the listening heap? Even if your demo is heard, what will make them want to take a chance on you? It's a matter of familiarity. The fact that the person may be an acquaintance or the fact that you have a friend who can introduce or recommend you to important people are big plusses in possibly getting hired. A wise gentleman once told me, "You are only one person away from meeting someone who may be important to your career." The better-known adage is, "It's not just what you know, but who you know."

Making Business Friendships

Networking is the process of meeting people; moreover, meeting people who may be an integral part of your career. I've got to tell you, I am not too fond of the word "networking." The way it is used today reeks of the image of people trying to meet with others only because they want something. I prefer the phrase "making business friendships." Ooh, I love the sound of that so much I've got to say it again: *"making business friendships."* To me, that's what it is all about—developing relationships. I don't want to get into a big long thing about the ins and outs of networking. Truth be told, there are books out there that get into a lot more detail than I'm willing or able to do. I can, however, share with you some of the things that I have done over the years.

Generally, I find that industry people prefer not to always talk about industry matters. So when I meet someone new, I try to talk about things other than music. The goal is to find a neutral subject that is of interest to us both. When first meeting someone I also recommend staying away from politics or religion as subject matter. Those two areas of discussion are usually debate starters. That is probably not a good way to start a conversation with someone unless you know for sure that the person has an affinity toward those types of conversations. Try to find some sort of "meaningful small talk" (now there's an oxymoron) to start off with.

A number of years back, I was invited to a major Recording Academy event. Once there, I must have spoken to at least 30 or so people and at night's end went home with a huge stack of business cards. About a week later, I decided to call some of those people whom I'd met. All those cards were neatly put into a flip business card holder that I had bought a day after the event. As I thumbed through the holder, I began to feel much the way one feels when walking into a lot full of parked cars. I suddenly felt indifferent. By that I mean, with no reference to the individuals who own each car, the fact that the cars are there is meaningless information. When you receive a business card from anyone, write on the back of it when and where you met that person. Also include what your conversation was about. When it's time to make contact with those individuals, you won't feel like you're in a parking lot of meaningless business cards.

Here's a tip for all those who use PDAs (i.e., personal digital assistants, such as the Palm handhelds, Treo 700, Blackberry, etc.): Most PDAs offer the ability to set up a master contact file of your information that can be beamed via infrared or Bluetooth from your PDA to someone else's PDA. Before each event I attend, I include in the comments section of my contact information the phrase, "We met at (the name of the event)," so that when I beam my information to an individual I have also given them a point of reference. I attach a short version of my bio to the master contact as well (see Figure 4.1).

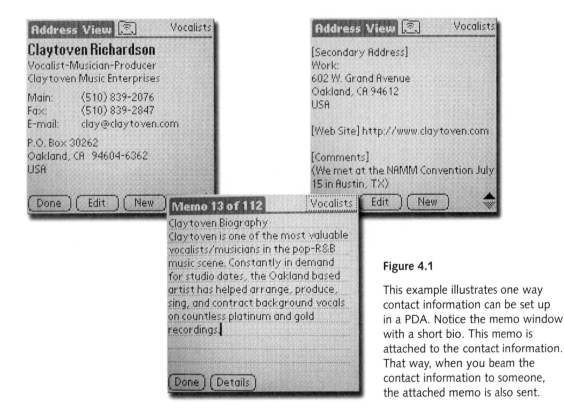

Figure 4.1

This example illustrates one way contact information can be set up in a PDA. Notice the memo window with a short bio. This memo is attached to the contact information. That way, when you beam the contact information to someone, the attached memo is also sent.

If someone beams me contact information, I immediately put into the comments section the same phrase as mentioned previously—"We met at (the name of the event)"—to avoid an electronic parking lot, which can sometimes be a bigger headache than the paper version.

Again I say, do not be afraid to speak up and introduce yourself. Most people in the music business aren't the self-centered, unapproachable divas that the media sometimes likes to portray. Try not to monopolize too much of their time with your conversation. Politely say the things that you need to say, listen for the things you need to listen for, gather the information you need to gather, and just as politely move on.

After any event, take a couple of days to input all of the information from business cards, notes written on napkins, etc., into your database. Now it's time to follow through with calls or e-mails to these people. Since you have written down the subject of your previous conversation, you will have a basis from which to start a new conversation.

Opportunities to Meet People

Where do you find industry people? That is another question that comes my way quite regularly. Well, the reality is that everywhere is a perfect place to network—or rather *make business friendships*. I once had to go to an auto shop to have some new tires put on my car. The salesman was a really nice guy, and we started to converse about a lot of different things while he was trying to locate the right tires in inventory. He finally set things up for my tires to be replaced, but I was going to have to come back in an hour to pick up my car. So, I gave the salesman my business card and wrote my cell phone number on the back for him to contact me if there were any problems. From my business card, he noticed that I was a singer. We wound up in another conversation, this time about the music business. Turned out that his cousin was a producer who was looking for someone to sing a couple of parts on a project. He hooked me up with his cousin, and I ended up getting what turned out to be a very good gig. Keep your mind open. You never know when or where opportunity may strike. The shoe salesman who just sold you a new pair of kicks may be friends with or related to the president of an advertising agency. The lady you just sold some cosmetics to may turn out to be the wife of a producer you have been trying to reach.

Don't rule out your friends and family either. This *is* the area where you can literally hand out a demo to everyone you know. If that's too costly, e-mail them an mp3 file. In the beginning stages of your career, friends and family are usually your best promotional team.

In addition to the people you meet in everyday life, there are some specific places and events that lend themselves to making business friendships. Some of these places and events include going to trade shows and conventions, participating in professional organizations' events, and doing public performances.

Trade Shows

Again, a trade show or convention is a large gathering of manufacturers of a particular classification of products. Conventions are usually 3 to 5 days long, with all types of exhibits, seminars, showcases, and much more. There are a great many music industry-oriented trade shows and conventions. Check in the Appendix for a list of some of the yearly trade shows and what they're all about. These trade shows are your opportunity to learn new things about the music business, check out new products, meet potential new clients, and meet with some of your peers. Don't forget to take some of your promotional materials—at minimum your business cards.

Professional Organizations

You should have a good list of trade organizations and the individual contacts at those organizations. You've at least checked out the list of trade organizations I've provided in the Appendix, right? If you haven't done so already, take a moment now to check out the list.

Many of these trade organizations put on or sponsor industry gatherings, shows, seminars, etc. Some of these events are a great place to showcase your talent. Call the appropriate contacts to see if there are events where they may let you perform. Just like trade shows, this is the perfect time to not only learn a bit more about the music industry from the professionals who attend, but also a great time to meet some of these professionals.

Public Performances

Many of my recording session jobs have come from clients seeing me perform with a band at concerts or shows. A live performance is a great way to showcase your talent. If you do not have a band that you can sing with, join a choir. Find as many opportunities as you can to sing in public. Create an e-mail sign-up list for your performances, and ask people to take part. If you have a Web site (highly recommended), make sure to mention that as well.

Newsletters and the Web

Take advantage of the mailing list that you're developing. Put together a newsletter to inform everyone of what is going on with your career. Come up with interesting stories that you can share. Make the newsletter personal. You want it to sound as if you are talking to one person. Make sure that printed versions of e-mails include your contact information.

If you've concentrated on collecting e-mail addresses, then an e-mail newsletter will be a better bet. The biggest advantage is that e-mail does not require postage. My newsletters are always addressed directly to the individuals receiving them and always include that person's first name in the salutation. I also periodically send e-mails about events in which they may have an interest. If you've put together a Web site, direct people to an area of your site that gives them an opportunity to hear or see your demo.

A Web site is the perfect spot to showcase your talents. One important thing to know about a Web site is that it is just a billboard. It doesn't let the world know that it exists. That's your job. Aside from making sure that your Web site address is displayed on every piece of printed material you send out, you have to let people know via word of mouth and any other way you can think of. In every situation that avails itself, be sure to mention your Web site.

Sending Out Your Demo

During your initial encounters, you will meet people who will be curious about your skills and who may want you to immediately send them a demo package. If you don't happen to have one on hand at the time, make sure that you get one out as soon as possible. There is another old saying that my parents used to tell me and my siblings, "Out of sight, out of mind"—and "the sooner the better"—also applies when you get a call from someone requesting a demo package.

Make sure that your demo package is well put together. Long before they get a chance to hear your demo, people will be affected by the appearance of your package and enclosed materials. Include a nicely drafted letter, preferably on your letterhead, that encapsulates the conversation that you had with that person.

Oh yeah, before I forget, never send out your package with codicils. "Here is my demo, but the second song is not mixed the way I want it yet" or "Here, let me write down the number where I can be reached because the one on my letterhead has changed" are just a couple of the things you should not say. If everything with your package is not right, then don't give it out. When you say these things to people, you are already starting off giving your demo a negative spin.

Lastly, never send out your demos unsolicited. You're at home in the middle of dinner and a stranger knocks on your door. You open the door and this person proceeds to try to sell you something. Not only is the person disturbing your peace and quiet (predicated on how loud you eat), but he is trying to sell you something that you don't need or want. That's exactly what you're doing when you send someone a demo that they didn't request. A lot of people will even return your package unopened. If you really want to send them a demo, call first and get permission.

Putting Together a Team

Do as much as you can yourself, but there are times when you will need the expertise of someone else. Look for a good graphic artist, a printer, a photographer, a lawyer, a manager, a publicist, or any other expert you may need. Find someone who is not only willing to work with you, but believes in you as well. Ask other singers and musicians for referrals to the people that they have worked with.

Now it's up to you to get it going. Make good use of all of your promotional tools. No one can champion your cause better than you. Find every way you can to get out there and make yourself known. If you see someone trying a promotional technique that you think is a good idea, don't be afraid to make it your own. Most people get hung up with fear—fear of rejection, fear of failure. Although fear is a healthy emotion that keeps us aware of things we should be careful of, do not succumb to fear. As I said, you may hear phrases like, "We regret to inform you…" or "Not interested" a lot before you get that first hiring call. So fear not, and go for it!

Taking Care of Business

So far this book has walked you through the process of becoming a professional vocalist in much the same way as you would do in a real-world setting. Now, however, I'm going to jump ahead of this process for a bit to talk about *labor unions*.

Labor Union: An organized association of workers, often in a trade or profession, formed to protect and further the rights and interests of its members.

LABOR UNIONS

The time to find out about labor unions is not after you have been hired for a gig. That's too late. Not having an understanding of what these organizations do and their effects on you could be the thing that prevents you from being able to accept certain types of gigs. Find out now what the unions are all about, how they can help you, and how (and when) you should go about joining. Take a look at the two unions that affect studio singers the most.

AFTRA and SAG

The American Federation of Television and Radio Artists (AFTRA) is a trade (performers) union that represents actors, radio and television announcers and newspersons, singers, and dancers in a broad range of entertainment and news media, including:

Broadcast, Public, and Cable Television—News, sports, weather, drama, comedy, soap operas, talk and variety shows, documentaries, children's programming, and reality and game shows

Radio—News, commercials, and hosted programs

Sound Recordings—CDs, singles, Broadway cast albums, and audio books

Non-Broadcast and Industrial Projects

Internet and Digital Programming

AFTRA currently has well over 80,000 members in 32 affiliated locals in major cities throughout the United States. The two largest locals are in Los Angeles, California, and New York, New York. (Current locals are listed under "Trade Organizations" in the Appendix.)

The second labor union that at some point will become important for you to become acquainted with is the Screen Actors Guild (SAG). Established in 1933, and now with 20 branches nationwide, SAG represents nearly 120,000 actors in:

Film

Television

Commercials

Interactive and Music Videos

So, what does an actors' union have to do with singers? Well, if you sing on a film sound track or in a national television commercial under a SAG agreement, you become a part of the cast and as such are entitled to certain payments. You may have also noticed a bit of overlap in the areas of coverage between AFTRA and SAG. Believe me, they have their jurisdictional issues worked out. For instance, AFTRA covers local and regional television commercials, while SAG covers national television commercials.

Union Functions

The main focus of both unions is to negotiate on behalf of its members *collective bargaining* agreements with production companies, record companies, advertising agencies, and so on. These agreements are a guarantee of *scale* pay rates, safe working conditions, and health and retirement benefits. Once a company signs the agreement with the union, it becomes a *signatory*. It is then the responsibility of the signatory to abide by all of the terms in the collective bargaining agreement. Further, it is the union's job to enforce that agreement. When AFTRA and SAG are unable to resolve disputes with employers, their contracts include procedures for binding *arbitration*. Unions pay for the costs of these proceedings.

Collective Bargaining: When an organized body of employees (a union) engages in the process of negotiating wages and other conditions of employment with an employer.

Scale: Minimum wage rate(s) or forms of compensation for union employees and contractors as specified in union agreements for specific types of employees or specific types of work.

Signatory: A company or entity that has signed a contract or letter of agreement with the union agreeing to terms regarding wages and working conditions for the members of that union.

Arbitration: The use of a neutral party (usually a judge) to resolve a dispute.

Union Benefits

Both AFTRA and SAG provide many benefits and programs for their members. Some benefits, such as the following, are common to both unions.

* Employer-paid health and retirement plans for members and their dependents that qualify. The Health Fund provides comprehensive medical and hospital benefits, a dental plan, a prescription drug program, and mental health and substance abuse programs.

* Access to credit union services (viz., the AFTRA–SAG Federal Credit Union and the Actors Federal Credit Union).

Other benefits are more specific to a particular union...

In the case of AFTRA:

* A series of supplemental benefits, discounts, and other programs through groups such as Group Benefits Associates, *TEIGIT*, UnionPlus/Union Privilege, and *MusicPro*.

* Scholarships are available to AFTRA members and dependents through the AFTRA Heller Memorial Foundation. AFTRA members are also eligible for assistance through organizations such as Theatre Authority and the Actors' Fund. In addition, several AFTRA locals sponsor scholarship programs and various charitable foundations for the benefit of AFTRA members and/or their dependents.

And in the case of SAG:

* The SAG Conservatory offers a variety of workshops taught by industry pros who will assess and enhance your skills as an actor.

* Casting workshops. Cold reading and scene showcases with working casting directors.

✳ The SAG Foundation. The charitable arm of the Guild offers member-only programs such as financial planning, career seminars, film screenings, and conversations with well-known actors.

TEIGIT: The Entertainment Industry Group Insurance Trust was founded in 1965 in an effort to provide affordable insurance for actors and musicians by devising a system that allows members of guilds to join together to get group rates.

MusicPro: A company that offers insurance coverage for instruments and equipment, studio liability, tour liability, travel accident, health insurance, life insurance, and long-term care.

When to Join

You can join AFTRA at anytime, but I recommend that you wait until you have performed or intend to perform professional work that is covered by AFTRA. At that point you are "officially" ready for membership. Another good reason to wait for the right time is the initial joining fee. The membership fee as of this writing was $1,300. There are also dues billed to the members semi-annually. The dues amount is based upon the member's AFTRA earnings during the previous year, with the minimum dues amount being $63.90 for members who earned less than $2,000.

SAG requirements are a bit different. There are two ways to join SAG: (1) show proof of SAG employment, or (2) show that you are already a member in good standing of an affiliate performance union like AFTRA or AGVA (American Guild of Variety Artists). The SAG membership fee is $1,432. As with AFTRA, SAG has semi-annual dues: $50, plus 1.85% of a performer's yearly SAG income.

I suggest that you do as many non-union gigs as you can before joining either of these unions to gain that much-needed professional experience, and to get yourself ready to be competitive with other union members.

The Taft–Hartley Act (Right to Work)

In the beginning, unless you are one of the lucky few, you will do a lot of non-union gigs. At some point, however, a union job opportunity might arise before you've become a member. It used to be that you could not work a union job unless you first became a union member, but the passage of the *Taft–Hartley Act* now gives performers the right to work one union job without first joining the union. However, after a minimum period of time on the job or upon working another job, you become what's called a "must join," meaning that at that point you must join the union in order to continue working union jobs. This is called "union shop" rules.

The other thing that the Taft–Hartley Act does is allow individual states to outlaw the union shop rules within its jurisdiction. A great many states have adopted "open shop" rules, which means an employee has "the right to work" for an employer that may be a union signatory without being forced to join that union. I have my own opinion about this; however, this is not the forum for expressing my political views. Suffice it to say that there are currently 22 "right-to-work" states (see Figure 5.1).

Taft–Hartley Act: A federal law that permits a non-union performer to work for a union signatory, under a union contract, for a period of 30 days. After that time the performer must join the union in order to accept any additional union work.

Figure 5.1

There are currently 22 "right-to-work" states.

Right To Work States

Once You Join

Make it your immediate business to sit down with a representative from the union you join and have him go over in detail the regulations that you have to follow. Also see if you can get together with an experienced union member to help you through the initial learning curve. Soak in all of the information that you can to maximize your membership.

Member Reports

When performing for a union recording session, there are no contracts to negotiate. Remember, the union has already done that for you and has established standards to which an employer has to adhere. Even though there is no contract that a singer takes to a session, in both unions a member on a union job fills out a member report. The member report is a record of what took place at a recording session—things such as who the session was for, the *call time*, the hours worked, the number of songs worked on, the number of tracks (*sides* when doing a sound recording) recorded, how much the singers are owed, and other pertinent information. The union uses this report to make sure that the performers are paid correctly. For every type of union job, there is a different member report, so while you're at it, also ask that same rep or union member to show you how to fill out member reports.

Call Time: The time a performer is scheduled to arrive at a recording session.

Side: Each track recorded (counting each overdub, multi-track, etc., as an additional side). This term is used mostly when dealing with union record (or as they say, phonograph) projects.

Employee Forms

Most people have at one point or another had a "regular job." So, you have likely filled out at least one set of employee forms. Well, just imagine that every time you do a union job you have to fill out these forms. If you have 20 different union jobs, you will have to fill out 20 sets of employee forms. If they aren't filled out correctly, you either get paid the wrong amount or, worse yet, you don't get paid at all, so it becomes easy to see the importance of knowing how to fill out this paperwork.

The two main forms that you will encounter are:

✳ **W-4 (Employee's Withholding Allowance Certificate).** This is a federal tax form from the Internal Revenue Service used by an employer to determine the amount of deductions that should be taken from an employee's paycheck. It lists your name, address, marital status, Social Security number, and the number of tax allowances you are claiming. (See Figure 5.2. For more information, visit http://www.irs.gov/.)

✶ **I-9 (Employment Eligibility Verification).** This is a federal form from the U.S. Citizenship and Immigration Services (a bureau of the U.S. Department of Homeland Security) used by employers to verify an employee's citizenship and legal eligibility to work in this country. (See Figure 5.3. For more information, visit http://www.uscis.gov/.) The employer is responsible for providing this form and having you fill it out; however, I make it a habit to bring both a pre-filled-in I-9 and W-4 to recording sessions. You should also bring your passport, or your driver's license and Social Security card. Your employer will need to see them and you will need them to complete the I-9.

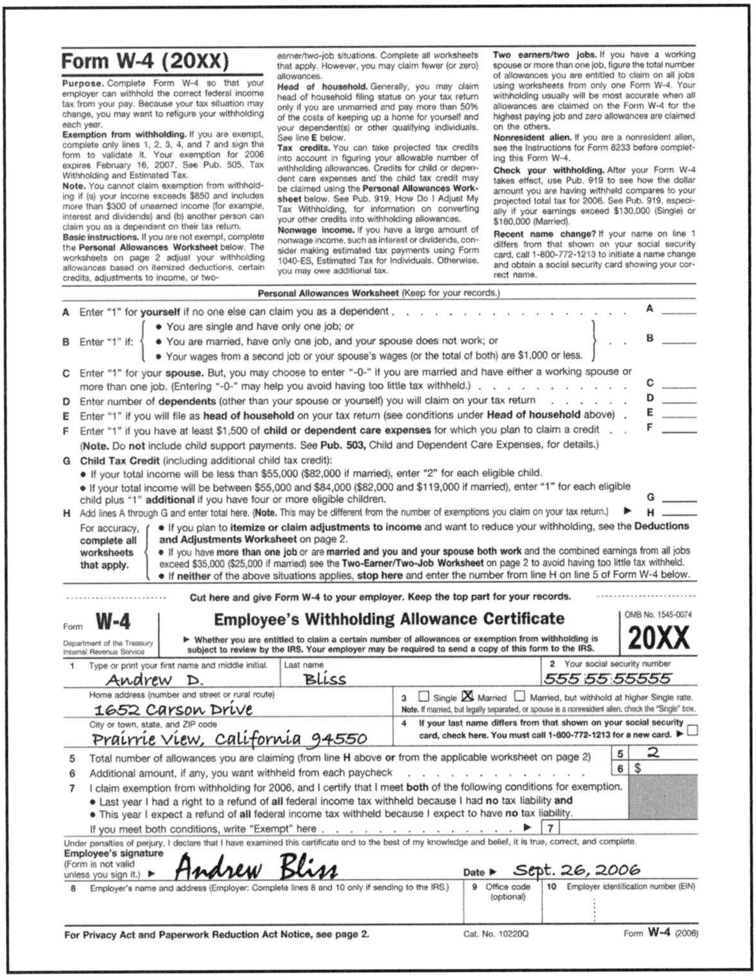

Form W-4 (20XX)

Purpose. Complete Form W-4 so that your employer can withhold the correct federal income tax from your pay. Because your tax situation may change, you may want to refigure your withholding each year.

Exemption from withholding. If you are exempt, complete only lines 1, 2, 3, 4, and 7 and sign the form to validate it. Your exemption for 2006 expires February 16, 2007. See Pub. 505, Tax Withholding and Estimated Tax.

Note. You cannot claim exemption from withholding if (a) your income exceeds $850 and includes more than $300 of unearned income (for example, interest and dividends) and (b) another person can claim you as a dependent on their tax return.

Basic instructions. If you are not exempt, complete the **Personal Allowances Worksheet** below. The worksheets on page 2 adjust your withholding allowances based on itemized deductions, certain credits, adjustments to income, or two-earner/two-job situations. Complete all worksheets that apply. However, you may claim fewer (or zero) allowances.

Head of household. Generally, you may claim head of household filing status on your tax return only if you are unmarried and pay more than 50% of the costs of keeping up a home for yourself and your dependent(s) or other qualifying individuals. See line **E** below.

Tax credits. You can take projected tax credits into account in figuring your allowable number of withholding allowances. Credits for child or dependent care expenses and the child tax credit may be claimed using the **Personal Allowances Worksheet** below. See Pub. 919, How Do I Adjust My Tax Withholding, for information on converting your other credits into withholding allowances.

Nonwage income. If you have a large amount of nonwage income, such as interest or dividends, consider making estimated tax payments using Form 1040-ES, Estimated Tax for Individuals. Otherwise, you may owe additional tax.

Two earners/two jobs. If you have a working spouse or more than one job, figure the total number of allowances you are entitled to claim on all jobs using worksheets from only one Form W-4. Your withholding usually will be most accurate when all allowances are claimed on the Form W-4 for the highest paying job and zero allowances are claimed on the others.

Nonresident alien. If you are a nonresident alien, see the Instructions for Form 8233 before completing this Form W-4.

Check your withholding. After your Form W-4 takes effect, use Pub. 919 to see how the dollar amount you are having withheld compares to your projected total tax for 2006. See Pub. 919, especially if your earnings exceed $130,000 (Single) or $180,000 (Married).

Recent name change? If your name on line 1 differs from that shown on your social security card, call 1-800-772-1213 to initiate a name change and obtain a social security card showing your correct name.

Personal Allowances Worksheet (Keep for your records.)

A Enter "1" for **yourself** if no one else can claim you as a dependent . . . . . A ____

B Enter "1" if:
- You are single and have only one job; or
- You are married, have only one job, and your spouse does not work; or
- Your wages from a second job or your spouse's wages (or the total of both) are $1,000 or less. . . B ____

C Enter "1" for your **spouse.** But, you may choose to enter "-0-" if you are married and have either a working spouse or more than one job. (Entering "-0-" may help you avoid having too little tax withheld.) . . . C ____

D Enter number of **dependents** (other than your spouse or yourself) you will claim on your tax return . . . D ____

E Enter "1" if you will file as **head of household** on your tax return (see conditions under **Head of household** above) . E ____

F Enter "1" if you have at least $1,500 of **child or dependent care expenses** for which you plan to claim a credit . . F ____
(**Note.** Do **not** include child support payments. See **Pub. 503,** Child and Dependent Care Expenses, for details.)

G **Child Tax Credit** (including additional child tax credit):
- If your total income will be less than $55,000 ($82,000 if married), enter "2" for each eligible child.
- If your total income will be between $55,000 and $84,000 ($82,000 and $119,000 if married), enter "1" for each eligible child plus "1" **additional** if you have four or more eligible children. G ____

H Add lines A through G and enter total here. (**Note.** This may be different from the number of exemptions you claim on your tax return.) ▶ H ____

For accuracy, **complete all worksheets that apply.**
- If you plan to **itemize or claim adjustments to income** and want to reduce your withholding, see the **Deductions and Adjustments Worksheet** on page 2.
- If you have **more than one job** or are **married and you and your spouse both work** and the combined earnings from all jobs exceed $35,000 ($25,000 if married) see the **Two-Earner/Two-Job Worksheet** on page 2 to avoid having too little tax withheld.
- If **neither** of the above situations applies, **stop here** and enter the number from line H on line 5 of Form W-4 below.

Cut here and give Form W-4 to your employer. Keep the top part for your records.

Form **W-4** — Department of the Treasury, Internal Revenue Service

Employee's Withholding Allowance Certificate

▶ **Whether you are entitled to claim a certain number of allowances or exemption from withholding is subject to review by the IRS. Your employer may be required to send a copy of this form to the IRS.**

OMB No. 1545-0074 **20XX**

1 Type or print your first name and middle initial. Andrew D. — Last name Bliss

2 Your social security number 555 55 55555

Home address (number and street or rural route) 1652 Carson Drive

3 ☐ Single ☒ Married ☐ Married, but withhold at higher Single rate.
Note. If married, but legally separated, or spouse is a nonresident alien, check the "Single" box.

City or town, state, and ZIP code Prairrie View, California 94550

4 **If your last name differs from that shown on your social security card, check here. You must call 1-800-772-1213 for a new card.** ▶ ☐

5 Total number of allowances you are claiming (from line **H** above **or** from the applicable worksheet on page 2) 5 2

6 Additional amount, if any, you want withheld from each paycheck . . . 6 $

7 I claim exemption from withholding for 2006, and I certify that I meet **both** of the following conditions for exemption.
- Last year I had a right to a refund of **all** federal income tax withheld because I had **no** tax liability **and**
- This year I expect a refund of **all** federal income tax withheld because I expect to have **no** tax liability.

If you meet both conditions, write "Exempt" here . . . ▶ 7

Under penalties of perjury, I declare that I have examined this certificate and to the best of my knowledge and belief, it is true, correct, and complete.

Employee's signature (Form is not valid unless you sign it.) ▶ Andrew Bliss — **Date** ▶ Sept. 26, 2006

8 Employer's name and address (Employer: Complete lines 8 and 10 only if sending to the IRS.) — 9 Office code (optional) — 10 Employer identification number (EIN)

For Privacy Act and Paperwork Reduction Act Notice, see page 2. Cat. No. 10220Q Form **W-4** (2006)

Figure 5.2

A federal form W-4 filled in by the employee.

U.S. Department of Justice
Immigration and Naturalization Service

OMB No. 1115-0136

Employment Eligibility Verification

Please read instructions carefully before completing this form. The instructions must be available during completion of this form. ANTI-DISCRIMINATION NOTICE: It is illegal to discriminate against work eligible individuals. Employers CANNOT specify which document(s) they will accept from an employee. The refusal to hire an individual because of a future expiration date may also constitute illegal discrimination.

Section 1. Employee Information and Verification. To be completed and signed by employee at the time employment begins.

Print Name: Last Bliss, First Andrew Middle Initial Maiden Name

Address *(Street Name and Number)* 1652 Carson Drive Apt. # Date of Birth *(month/day/year)* Dec. 15, 1962

City Prairie View, State California Zip Code 94550 Social Security # 555-55-5555

I am aware that federal law provides for imprisonment and/or fines for false statements or use of false documents in connection with the completion of this form.

I attest, under penalty of perjury, that I am (check one of the following):
☒ A citizen or national of the United States
☐ A Lawful Permanent Resident (Alien # A________)
☐ An alien authorized to work until __/__/__ (Alien # or Admission #)________

Employee's Signature Andrew Bliss Date *(month/day/year)* Sept. 26, 2006

Preparer and/or Translator Certification. *(To be completed and signed if Section 1 is prepared by a person other than the employee.) I attest, under penalty of perjury, that I have assisted in the completion of this form and that to the best of my knowledge the information is true and correct.*

Preparer's/Translator's Signature Print Name

Address *(Street Name and Number, City, State, Zip Code)* Date *(month/day/year)*

Section 2. Employer Review and Verification. **To be completed and signed by employer. Examine one document from List A OR examine one document from List B and one from List C, as listed on the reverse of this form, and record the title, number and expiration date, if any, of the document(s)**

	List A	OR	List B	AND	List C
Document title:	Passport		Driver's License		Social Security #
Issuing authority:	USA		California		
Document #:	55-5555		N555555		555-55-5555
Expiration Date *(if any)*:	12 15 09		12 15 10		__/__/__
Document #:					
Expiration Date *(if any)*:	__/__/__				

CERTIFICATION - I attest, under penalty of perjury, that I have examined the document(s) presented by the above-named employee, that the above-listed document(s) appear to be genuine and to relate to the employee named, that the employee began employment on *(month/day/year)* __/__/__ **and that to the best of my knowledge the employee is eligible to work in the United States. (State employment agencies may omit the date the employee began employment.)**

Signature of Employer or Authorized Representative Print Name Title

Business or Organization Name Address *(Street Name and Number, City, State, Zip Code)* Date *(month/day/year)*

Section 3. Updating and Reverification. To be completed and signed by employer.

A. New Name *(if applicable)* B. Date of rehire *(month/day/year) (if applicable)*

C. If employee's previous grant of work authorization has expired, provide the information below for the document that establishes current employment eligibility.

Document Title:______ Document #:______ Expiration Date (if any): __/__/__

I attest, under penalty of perjury, that to the best of my knowledge, this employee is eligible to work in the United States, and if the employee presented document(s), the document(s) I have examined appear to be genuine and to relate to the individual.

Signature of Employer or Authorized Representative Date *(month/day/year)*

Form I-9 (Rev. 11-21-91)N Page 2

Figure 5.3

A federal form I-9 filled in by the employee. In Section 2 of this example, Lists A, B, and C are filled out, but in a real-world setting, you will only have to fill out either List A or List B and C.

Other Things to Know about Union Payment

What is the scale rate for a job? The amount of a scale payment is predicated on the type of job, the number of people involved, and sometimes the number of *tracks* that you sing or the length of the song. For example, a group of four background vocalists hired for an AFTRA sound recording session would each receive a minimum of $166.00 for a 2-hour session. If the song were longer than 3:30, the compensation for each singer would be $332.00. For the same type of job and the same amount of time, a lead vocalist would earn $366.50. However, an off-camera lead singer for an AFTRA interactive media project would receive a minimum of $716.00 for a 4-hour day. It can be a bit confusing, so I recommend visiting www.aftra.org and www.sag.org for more about union scale rates.

Though the union has worked out a minimum compensation for a session, it is only the minimum. Over a span of years, some singers have worked their way into getting *overscale* payments for sessions. Also, if you work between the hours of 12 A.M. and 8 A.M., or if you work on New Year's Day, Memorial Day, July 4th, Labor Day, Thanksgiving, or Christmas, you're entitled to premium pay, which is an additional 50% of the scale rate. A vocalist can also receive a residual payment in addition to the scale pay for a session. This residual payment, also known as a reuse fee or replay fee, is due a performer each time a television show, commercial, etc. is rebroadcast or re-*aired*. Many times I am asked, "Do background singers get royalties from records?" In a way, the answer is yes. A contingency scale payment is an additional payment made to non-royalty AFTRA artists whose performances are included on commercially released recordings. The amount of earnings paid is "contingent" upon the number of recordings sold.

Anytime there is a background vocal session that includes three or more singers, there must be a contractor (or session leader). The contractor is the person who acts as the coordinator or leader of a recording session for a music producer or record company. Duties can include contacting the singers, conducting singers and rehearsals, minor rearranging of vocal parts, or any other similar supervisory duties. The contractor is most often one of the singers on the session and also has the duty of filling out and turning in member reports. There is extra pay for this job, though in my experiences as a contractor, it's not enough—especially when the job calls for some baby-sitting.

Track: In recording, a discrete or distinguishable strip or path along the length of a magnetic tape (or a segment of a computer hard drive), on which data or sound can be recorded and played back separately from the other tracks on the tape (or computer hard drive).

Overscale: When a vocalist receives more than minimum union scale for work on a project.

Air: To broadcast on radio or television.

Royalty Artist: A person who is compensated for his or her services as a recording artist by royalties paid on each unit (records, CDs, cassettes, etc.) manufactured, distributed, and/or sold.

NON-UNION WORK

Let's face the fact that in this dawn of the independent record label era, a lot of work out there is non-union. Some of these jobs can be very lucrative; however, one of the biggest dichotomies between a union and a non-union gig is *you* doing all of the negotiating. Following are some key things to remember when trying to settle on terms for a gig.

What to Charge

Payment is sometimes based on your skill level and what the client is hiring you to do. For most non-union sessions, I recommend charging at least the minimum of what a singer would make if the session were union. Most often I charge more, since these sessions are usually on a *flat fee*, or *buy-out* status. Buy-outs from a union's standpoint are a no-no, but from the point of view of a singer trying to earn his or her stripes, it could be the very thing that launches that singer's studio career. You will have to weigh each situation as it occurs.

Flat Fee/Buy Out: A one-time fee, usually paid up front, for the privilege of obtaining a license or the retention of professional services, as opposed to royalties, wages, or other forms of continuing compensation.

Another issue to consider when negotiating your pay for the session is the way the rate is calculated. It could be either by the hour or by the song. A lot of clients will oftentimes opt to pay you by the song. Sometimes it's a little more affordable (so they think) for them to pay that way. That is fine as long as the amount per song is comfortable to you. However, there is one tricky thing to consider regarding a by-the-song rate. You should always negotiate a time limit per song—say, two hours max per song—and for any time over that maximum, the employer must pay an additional per-hour rate. The reason is simple: Without putting any time restrictions on the session, it's conceivable to wind up spending numerous hours at a studio just to record a song that takes you only an hour to sing, or spending hours singing on one song with no extra compensation. You could find yourself in the awkward position of trying to negotiate for extra money after you've already done the work. Good luck with that!

Agreements

If I know the producer very well, he or she knows how I like to work and how things have to be for me to work on the session. For those producers who are new to me, I put together a little agreement that states what our understanding is with regards to the recording session. Take a look at Figure 5.4 for an example of the "Vocalist Letter Agreement" that I sometimes use. This is a basic personal service agreement.

 Disclaimer Regarding Sample Vocalist Agreement: Claytoven Richardson, Claytoven Music, and Thomson Course Technology make no warranties or representations in connection with this document. This document is for informational use only. Laws and procedures change frequently and can be interpreted differently by different people. For specific advice geared to your specific situation, or if you have any legal questions regarding this document, *PLEASE, CONSULT WITH AN ATTORNEY*.

Even though I strongly recommend that you have all contracts constructed and read by a qualified attorney, it behooves you to at least have a basic understanding of personal service agreements. There are two basic types of service agreements. The first is an exclusive agreement, like that of a recording contract, where for a specific period of time a record company has exclusive rights to an artist's recording services. For a more in-depth look into recording artist agreements, I again recommend Michael Aczon's book, *The Professional Musician's Legal Companion*.

Then there are non-exclusive agreements, like the one in Figure 5.4, which deal with an employee's services for one specific job. These types of agreements do not prohibit the employee from doing the same service for someone else. They also have certain terms that are fairly common.

Example of a Vocalist Letter Agreement

(Date)

(Employer)
(Address)
(Address)
(Phone Number)

Dear (Employer),

This letter sets forth the terms of our agreement with respect to the payment of fees for the recording services of *(Vocalist Name)* (hereinafter referred to as "Me, My, or I") for the recording of the *(number of songs) (#)* selection(s) entitled: *"(Song Titles)"*.

In consideration of the foregoing, we agree as follows:

1. You agree to pay to me the sum of *(Amount)* Dollars *($00.00)* per selection in connection with the services performed during the session(s) dated *(date of session(s))*. Said sum shall not be treated as an advance against any future compensation. You and I shall keep an accurate accounting of all hours spent during the session(s) and attach a written accounting to this agreement after the session(s).

2. You further agree that, in the event any or all of the recordings are released commercially (whether in their original state or following additional recording, re-mastering, or performances), you shall pay to me an additional amount equal to AFTRA union scale for such services. Such additional compensation shall be paid to me through AFTRA, provided that my performances are used on the released masters.

3. The effective date of this letter agreement appears above.

4. Our relationship is that of independent contractor. This agreement shall not be construed to create a partnership between you and me.

5. This agreement constitutes the entire agreement between the parties, and supersedes all prior and contemporaneous agreements, understandings, negotiations, and discussions, whether oral or written.

6. The terms and provisions of this agreement shall be binding upon and inure to the benefit of our respective executors, administrators, successors and assigns.

7. If any legal action, arbitration or any other proceeding is brought for the interpretation or enforcement of this agreement because of any alleged dispute, breach, default or misrepresentation in connection with any provision of this agreement, the prevailing party shall be entitled to recover his or her attorneys' fees and costs incurred in such proceeding, together with any other relief to which the prevailing party may be entitled.

If the foregoing correctly sets forth your understanding of our agreement, please so indicate by signing in the space provided below and returning one (1) copy to me at my above address.

Sincerely,

(Vocalist Name)

by: _____

AGREED AND ACCEPTED:

(Employer)

by: _____

Figure 5.4

A sample Vocalist Letter Agreement.

Take a brief look at the terms of the Vocalist Letter Agreement, starting with the opening clause that states the parties involved and gives a general description of the employee's intended services. The next two clauses, labeled 1 and 2, deal with consideration. Consideration is when something is done or promised by one party in exchange for something done or promised by another. This is the essence of any agreement. Without consideration, there is no contract. In the Vocalist Letter Agreement, the employer promises a certain amount of compensation, and to deal with that compensation in a certain manner in return for the employee performing recording services on a set date. Other terms that can be put into the consideration section of this agreement include the method of payment (e.g., check, cash, money order, etc.), when the payment is due, call time for the session, how project credits are dealt with (more on project credits later), or the two hours per song maximum that I discussed earlier.

Paragraphs 3 through 7 of the agreement are called boilerplate clauses, which are standardized pieces of text common to most contracts:

Clause 3 sets the date of the agreement.

Clause 4 defines the relationship between the parties.

Clause 5 states that this is the entire agreement and that there is nothing further to be added to the contract, either written or oral. This clause further states that this agreement now takes precedence over any prior agreement.

Clause 6 states that responsibility of this agreement, as well as any benefits therefrom, can be passed on to heirs, administrators, executors of estates, and so on.

Clause 7 basically says that if a lawsuit or arbitration proceeding takes place to settle any dispute, breach, or argument dealing with this contract, whoever loses not only has to properly settle the dispute, but also has to pay the other party's attorney fees.

The final clause states the conditions under which the document is binding to the parties. Namely, it has to be signed by both parties and a copy has to be sent to the employee. Without the full execution (signed by both parties) of this agreement, this contract is meaningless.

And there you have it, a quick lesson on the structure of a personal service agreement. Additionally, however, there is still one big lesson to remember regarding any contract: A contract is only as good as the people signing it. If the person or company is untrustworthy, signing an agreement with them is not going to change that. You would just be setting yourself up for a lot of heartache and headaches. You would do well to try to find out as much as you can about that person or company before you sign any agreement. And again, by all means consult with an attorney.

Project Credits

Make no mistake: I want to get paid for what I do just like anybody else; however, the credits can be just as important, if not more important than the money. Some of the first recording sessions that I sang on were non-union. Even though the pay was barely decent, I didn't care. The credits were worth so much more money because of whom the sessions were for. I ended up getting a slew of gigs based on those album credits. Make sure that you discuss what the credits will be.

The Value of Negotiating

The non-union world of work requires you to be on top of your negotiating game. Producers try to be fair, but the reality in life is that you are the only person who is really going to look out for you. Years ago, I was flying to New York for a gig and was reading one of those airline magazines. (You know I was bored!) I came across an advertisement about a business seminar featuring Dr. Chester L. Karrass, a leading expert in demonstrating how to negotiate successfully. There in that ad was his mantra, which has stuck with me for years: "In business as in life, you don't get what you deserve, you get what you negotiate."

The Hiring Call

One of the happiest moments of my life was when I got my first call from a producer wanting to *book* me for a vocal recording session, though admittedly I was a bit perplexed as to why I was getting called to sing. Fortunately, that state of perplexity helped me to keep the exuberance that I was feeling in check long enough to have the initial business conversation. When the hiring call comes in, your demeanor should be friendly but also business oriented and professional. Be careful not to come off as arrogant. Before the conversation goes too far, politely ask if you can put the person on hold. Once you've done so, quickly grab a pad and pencil, scream out a backslapping, "YEAH!," and then immediately get back on the phone. Pay close attention to what the caller is saying and take plenty of notes (see Figure 6.1).

QUESTIONS YOU SHOULD ASK

Your hiring call could come from a producer, an engineer, the *A&R* director of a record company, an artist's manager, a representative of an advertising agency, or maybe even the artist. Whoever it is that calls, there are some specific questions you should be prepared to ask in an effort to make sure that the impending session is as successful as possible. Before you start to bombard the caller with a ton of questions, however, allow the person the opportunity to volunteer as much information as possible. Try to ask your questions only as a means to fill in the gaps.

Figure 6.1

Always take notes from the hiring call.

Book: (1) To schedule an appearance or make an appointment. (2) To engage a vocalist(s) and/or musician(s) for a performance. (3) To hire a studio or other facility for a recording or performance. (4) To reserve time.

A&R (Artist and Repertoire): The division of a record label that is responsible for scouting and developing talent. The A&R department is the liaison between the recording artist and the record company. Finding songwriters and record producers for the recording artist as well as scheduling recording sessions are often some of the duties of this department.

Where and When Is the Session?

This seems like an obvious thing to ask, yet with some of my earlier sessions I remember having to call on the day of a session to find out the address of the studio. Every time I had to do that I felt a bit stupid, so make sure you get the date, the time, and the location of the recording session. The Internet really makes things easy with regards to directions. Go to Yahoo Maps, MapQuest, or any of the many free online mapping services to get directions. Even if the caller gives you directions, double-check them with one of these services. The last excuse you want for being late is, "I got lost." Besides, we aren't supposed to be late anyway, right?

What Is the Session For?

Is this session for a demo project, for a record (there I go showing my age again), I mean CD project, a television or radio commercial, or a movie soundtrack? This information is important because it can help you determine whether or not this will be a union session. If it is a union session, you will need this information when filling in a *member report*.

Who Is the Session For?

Is there a recording artist or is this a demo session? If there is an artist, is the artist signed to a label or is this a production project? Is there a record company or advertising agency involved? If so, you want to try to get who they are and their address. Again, if it is a union session, you will need this information when filling in a member report.

What and When Do You Get Paid?

Is this a union or non-union session? If it is a union session, then (as you found in the previous chapter) a minimum pay structure (scale) is already set up. If not, you will need to know who is paying, how much you're getting paid, and when you get paid.

You might have noticed that I've broached the subject of pay almost last. Although the bottom line is that you're getting hired to do a job and you want to get paid for that job, you don't want the client to feel that your only interest in doing the session is getting paid.

Other Considerations

With some sessions, you may want to ask for a demo copy of the song(s) so that you have an opportunity to become familiar with the song(s) prior to the session. You may want the lyrics as well, especially if you are being hired to sing lead vocals.

Project credits were discussed in the last chapter but are worth talking about again. Union member reports have that aspect covered, but in the non-union world you should inquire about credits. Most often, credits are just as important, if not more important, than getting paid. Having album credits on a CD that winds up going *gold* or *platinum* would lend a considerable amount of credibility and marketability to you as a vocalist. Those credits could translate into you getting called for other sessions that you might not have been called for otherwise. Also keep track of release dates, airtimes, etc. This information could come in handy in a multitude of ways, including being used for your press releases, newsletters, bios, Web site, etc.

 Gold, Platinum: Part of a system enacted by the Recording Industry Association of America (RIAA) in 1958 to certify the sales of a sound recording. Gold status indicates the sale of 500,000 copies, while platinum status indicates the sale of 1,000,000 copies. The RIAA is a trade group that represents the United States recording industry.

Professionalism

Once you've mastered the art of getting the job, the hard part becomes trying to keep jobs. A big part of maintaining work is understanding that when someone pays you to sing, that becomes your job, even if it is fun. The mistake that some people make is that when they are at their "9 to 5" they act one way, but for some reason as soon as the work is music related, it seems as though all of their work ethics just sift from their heads like pulling a drain stopper from a sink. What I am trying to impress upon you is that, although you are performing musically, you can't afford to forget about the word "business" in the phrase "the music business." You must keep the same work ethics and etiquette in your music career as you would in any "9 to 5" job, and sometimes even more. So what elements of professionalism should you be aware of? What things should you do or not do?

ATTIRE

One of the first things to consider is your attire. If you were going to a job interview for a major corporate position, you wouldn't wear short pants and a T-shirt, would you? Don't laugh. I've seen it happen. Just as with any other "regular" job, you have to be cognizant of what the gig is about. You have to dress the part. I'm not saying to sacrifice that which makes up your style, but rather that you can impart some of who you are into what is appropriate attire for the job. Whenever applicable, ask if there is a dress code, especially when it comes to commercials or industrials. A lot of the time, the producer will not be the only one present at the recording session. Usually the client (e.g., an advertising agent, artist, record executive, etc.) is in attendance. Most of the time, the client makes judgments based not only on whether your vocals sound good, but also partially on your appearance. The client often determines whether you'll get hired for the next recording session, and the client is looking at things such as what you are wearing, whether you are smiling when you are singing about their product, and your overall conduct. So it is important to understand that if you are dressed inappropriately, the client's interpretation might be that you don't really care about the gig. It's just as if you dressed wrong for your "regular job." The supervisor's view is that you don't care about your appearance and, more importantly, about your job. Your supervisor might address you about your attire, but a client just might not call you back for another session.

Something else to consider with regards to your attire is the noise factor. Microphones in the studio are very sensitive listening devices (more about that later) that can pick up the sound of a nylon jacket rustling, the jingling of ear rings, or shoes that squeak when moving your feet to the beat. Most of the time, because you are singing in the studio while wearing headphones, you are not aware of the noises your clothes may be making until the recording engineer busts you on it. Take some time to check through the clothes you plan on wearing to the studio for their noise factor.

PUNCTUALITY

"The producer or the client can be late, but you can't." My singing buddies and I always laugh about that, but it is so true. Your first impression at the recording session, even before the producer or client sees or hears you, is made by your punctuality. If you are fortunate enough for someone to believe in your talent enough to hire you for a recording session, the one thing you cannot be is late. During my college marching band days, the band director had a saying that has stuck with me for years:

"To be early is to be on time.

To be on time is to be late.

To be late is just ridiculous."

Plan to arrive at a recording session at least 15 minutes before your scheduled arrival time. If you know that it will take an hour to get to the studio, leave an hour and a half before your scheduled arrival time. Inevitably, something always happens when you leave with just enough time to get there right on time: There's an accident on the freeway. You get a flat tire. Maybe there's some work being done on the road. The point is that when you make your travel plans based on getting there right on time, usually something happens to make you late, so be early to be on time.

It was not too far into my career when I found myself in New York singing background vocals on a major record project. While taking a break in the lounge, I ran across a producer, Geoff, who was an old friend of mine from college. We hung out together for a while, swapping old stories. Just before I had to go back into the studio, he asked me if I would be interested in doing a commercial session for him a few days from then and if so, could I be there at about 10 A.M. Two days later, there I was at that studio, my usual 15 minutes early. During those 15 minutes, Geoff showed up along with two singers, Laura and Tami. We started rehearsing promptly at 10 A.M. At about 11 A.M., another vocalist, Aaron showed up. Geoff seamlessly integrated him into the rehearsal. After a 5-minute break and being introduced to the client (the agent for a prominent advertising agency in New York), we started recording at 11:30 A.M. Things were going along great until about 12:15 P.M., when I saw that a gentleman had gone into the *control room* and had begun what looked like a very intense conversation with Geoff, right in front of the client. Without a second thought, Geoff told us over the *talkback* to take a break and go hang out in the lounge area for a while. After being in the lounge area for a short while, this same gentleman came into the room, steaming. One of the singers, Tami, said, "Hey Arthur! What happened?" But before the story could unfold, the engineer came in and told us that they were ready to get started again. We left Arthur in the lounge and went back into the studio. Our session ended at 1:30 P.M. that afternoon, but it would be days later before I would finally find out what had happened to Arthur at the studio.

 Control Room: A room separated from a studio area that contains the mixing console and recording equipment, and in which the engineer or producer oversees the recording of a performance.

Talkback: A communication device that links performers in the studio with a producer or engineer in the control room.

A week later I was back in the Bay Area getting ready to start my workday when I got a call from Geoff. He wanted to thank me for the job I did and let me know that the project came out great. More important, the client loved it and planned on using it in their next television commercial. Geoff also took the time to apologize for the mishap in the studio. Normally I wouldn't have asked what happened, but I felt that since we were friends that he wouldn't mind telling me. (Well, okay, I was just being nosey.) Apparently, Arthur, the second guy that arrived late was mad because Geoff had to fire him. Geoff went on to tell me, "Hey man, when Arthur didn't show up by 10:30 A.M. I had to make a call. I had a deadline of 1:30 P.M. that the client was insistent that I meet. I called Aaron, and he just happened to be in the area running errands and consented to do the gig. It was my behind on the line, so I had to do what I had to do." Lesson learned.

There are only a few things in this business that are worse than being late and that will get you fired faster than the time it took you to read this sentence. Well, maybe not quite that fast, but in Arthur's case, pretty close. When you're late you cause an avalanche of problems. Time is money—money that is being spent on studio time, an engineer, musicians, or possibly other vocalists, which in the end comes out of the client's pocket. Your tardiness also reflects badly in the client's eyes on the producer's ability to choose reliable personnel. So if all you remember from all of this is, "To be early is to be on time," and you conduct yourself accordingly, that will take you a long way.

CONDUCT BEFORE, DURING, AND AFTER THE SESSION

For every type of recording session there is a different type of protocol required to help make the session run smoothly. Proper conduct is an essential part of that protocol; however, there are things that people sometimes do that go against the grain. Granted, a great deal of people, myself included, got into the music business for the joy of it. The problem is that when you do a recording session you are "working" for someone. It's worth saying again that many people forget about the "business" in the phrase "the music business." I guess that a small part of the blame can fall partially on the music industry itself, as it is our job to perpetuate the good-time images the public sees in videos, TV shows, and the like. The reality is that a recording session is just like any other job and too much negative behavior and partying often results in people not getting called back for another recording session.

My father once told me that you learn more about a person by being quiet, listening and observing, than by talking. After singing on hundreds of recording sessions, I've watched other vocalists do all sorts of things to lose their gigs. After a while, I started to realize that a few of these behaviors were common. Some are so common that I gave many of these behaviors names. Following are a few bad behaviors with some accompanying antidotes:

The Chatterbox. *This individual talks too much during a session to the point of distraction.* This person is the chatty type who incessantly talks loud and continuously until finally someone, usually the producer, has to tell him or her to quiet down so that work can be done.

It's Party Time. *This person parties to the point of keeping every-one from doing their jobs.* This usually happens when there are people on the session who haven't seen each other for a while. One of them starts to feel that it's catch-up time. Then it's, "Hey man, how are you doing? I haven't seen you in a long time." "Yeah, how is your family doing? I heard that you are going back to school." And the conversation just goes on and on and on until the producer or the client finally has to say, "Can we get a little work done?" You have to pay attention to what is going on in the session, and more important, you need to keep up with where the producer or client is coming from. You have to have the discipline to be able to shut down the party.

Another version is the person who wants to play or tell jokes too much during the session. Either way, it's annoying and distracting to the producer and client. One point to make: While it is impor-tant to add a bit of socializing to the recording session, and telling jokes is sometimes a part of that socializing process, it is important to have the wherewithal and discipline to know when to turn it off.

Woe Is Me. *This person brings the "poor me" attitude to the session and kills the mood.* This one is my personal favorite. Here's an example: The producer asks, "How's it going?" The vocalist answers, "It's been a bad day. My girlfriend left me and the rent is due. I might have to sell my car." "Hey man, I'm sure things will be alright for you," says the producer, but now the producer is thinking, "Wow, I feel bad for the guy, but do I want this bad vibe on my client's project?" When you come to a session, you have to turn off all of the personal problems. You might be good enough to sing past your problems, but now you've already planted into the minds of the producer and client that this could be a depressing session at any moment. If you find that you are just having too hard of a time, you would do better to call (giving as much advance notice as possible) and postpone the session to another day if you can.

The Armchair Producer. *This person spends too much time trying to do the producer's job.* A singer's last words: "The vocal part is clashing with one of the guitar parts. I think you should take it out. Maybe you should consider redoing the music tracks. And what about that lead vocal? It's a little *sharp*." You may feel that the producer is not doing things the way that you're used to. The producer may not be doing things in a manner that you feel is musically correct. It doesn't matter. You cannot put the producer in the unenviable position of feeling like you're challenging his authority, especially in front of the client. A producer may sometimes be open to suggestions, but usually only if he asks. However, even if the producer asks, you should keep your comments to a minimum—after all, you're getting paid to sing, not to be a producer.

I Can't Hear Myself Think. *This is a derivative of "The Chatterbox,"* but in my opinion even worse. This usually happens when the vocalists are behind the microphone while in the studio. One or more of the vocalists starts The Chatterbox syndrome every time recording stops. The mistake is made when everyone thinks that the microphone is off between *takes*. Furthermore, while this bantering is taking place, it is interfering with decisions and discussions concerning the recording process that may be taking place in the control room. It is possible for the microphone to be *hot* even though you may not hear that it's on in your headphones. So when you are in the studio, you should always assume that the microphone is live.

A What? *This is someone whose lack of knowledge slows down the progress of the session.* It is important that you have at least a basic knowledge of the equipment that you'll be using and any other equipment that may be used in connection with the recording of your voice. If someone asks you if you like the *reverb* being used on your voice and your response is, "What?," that could be a problem. Engineers, producers, and other singers who have been recording for some time can recognize very quickly when a singer is overly "green." Now, on occasion there will be times when maybe everyone works in a way that is a little different from what you are used to. They may even have their own private set of terminology for things. However, you have to pay attention and try to catch on quickly. Your goal is to try not to be in the position of having everything explained to you.

Sharp: Playing an instrument or singing above the proper or indicated pitch.

Hot, Live: On.

Take: A version of a recorded performance.

Reverb: An electronic device used in recording to simulate natural ambience.

I Have Expectations. *This is someone who has an unrealistic view of what he should get from a recording session.* The best way to explain this is through a little story. I was hired to contract 10 singers for a record project. Everyone sang his or her tail off, and the producer was so pleased that he took us out for a sushi dinner at this really nice Japanese restaurant and told us to order whatever we wanted. Toward the end of the dinner, I caught a glimpse of the bill, and believe me when I tell you that he really showed his appreciation! Well, a few days later, during our next recording session with the same producer, it was getting close to time to take a lunch break when one of the singers said, "Ooh, I could sure use some sushi." A couple of the other singers and I sort of grimaced when we heard this; however, the producer was cool. He laughed it off and didn't say anything. The following week we had another session with the same producer and once again the same singer uttered the words, "Ooh, I could sure use some sushi." And once again the producer was gracious enough to let the comment slide by. Well, just before the next recording session, I got a call from the producer telling me not to invite that particular singer to any more recording sessions. I knew the reason, but I just wanted to hear him say the words. So he did, "That singer has too many expectations. I took you guys out for dinner being nice. I don't owe you that.... I pay you all good money to sing for my projects. For this person to keep asking me for dinner that way is annoying and I don't want to deal with it!"

The Gossip. *This individual talks too much about others' business.* Here's a little story called, "Be Careful of What You Say and Where You Say It": This particular recording session was in Los Angeles and involved me, two ladies (Beth and Ruth), and two other guys (Ben and Walker). In the middle of the session, the producer decided that on a particular part in the song he wanted only Beth and Ruth to sing. So he gave me and the other guys a break. Since I was the contractor for the session, I had to stay in the control room and watch the session while Ben and Walker went to relax in the lounge. Once the ladies finished the part that the producer wanted, he said that he was going to go get Ben and Walker so that we could finish up. A few minutes later the producer came back, but the guys weren't with him. I asked him if he had changed his mind. He said, "No, I just got distracted with some other things that I needed to do." I then told the producer that I would go get Ben and Walker. After a couple of hours, we finished the recording session and went home. A week later I got a call from the producer wanting to book another recording session, but this time he didn't want Walker on the session. Being the Curious George that I am, I asked him why. The producer told me, "The other day when I went to get the guys, before I could get all the way into the lounge area I could hear one of the guys talking. As I got closer, I realized that Walker was bad-mouthing Beth (one of the ladies on the session). Walker went on to say how he felt that Beth wasn't worthy of being on the session and that if left up to him, he would have picked somebody much better." The producer went on to say, "I just turned around and came back into the control room without letting the guys know that I was there. I normally would let that kind of stuff go except for two things: (1) Beth, the singer who Walker was talking about was the very person who got Walker the gig in the first place, and, (2) I got to thinking, what's to make me think that he wouldn't do the same thing to me behind my back." All I could say was, "Oh well!"

Will You Leave, Please. *This person finds it hard to leave after her job is done.* I made this mistake early in my career, fortunately not to my detriment. I did a lead vocal for a commercial session. When I finished, the producer and the client were very excited. So excited that I got caught up in the moment. Instead of making my exit and leaving on a high note, I decided that I wanted to hang out to see the rest of the recording process. Well, the producer and the client stalled as long as they could until the producer finally pulled me to the side and asked me as nicely as he could to leave. Apparently, there were some things that they needed to discuss, and it would have been inappropriate to do so in front of me. "Oops!"

> *You can't afford to forget about the word "business" in the phrase "the music business."*

I have a few others that are a bit more obvious. "I Can't Take You Nowhere" (bringing a guest to your recording session, which usually is a no-no) and "Your Ego Is Bigger Than Your Talent" are just a couple of other ways not to conduct yourself during a recording session. I know that you might be thinking, "This is all common sense." Well, you'd be surprised at how easy it is to get caught up in the moment. By all means, if there is a moment when you can have fun, go for it, but always be mindful that you've been hired to work.

Okay, I've had some fun talking about the "Don'ts"; now I want to talk about a couple of very important "Do's."

If You Are Wrong, Admit It. If you should do something that is out of place, admit to it and apologize. Likewise, if you sing the wrong note and get called on it, just politely say you're sorry and ask to try it again. Please stay away from the response phrase, "I know." That's an argument starter. Besides, you'll be surprised at the rise in respect you gain when you simply respond, "Sorry. My fault."

Try to Make Things Go as Easy as Possible. You should always try to be as cordial as possible, even when faced with a producer or client who is being indignant with you. The music business is a small world, and it is easy to get a bad reputation. Try to never burn a bridge. Remember what I told you earlier: You are only one person away from meeting someone who may be very important to your career. Murphy's Law says that the producer you went off on last week in the studio will turn out to be that "one person." Also, careers recycle somewhat like the hydrologic cycle, so do your best to remember that the people you meet while going up are the same people you're likely to meet when coming down.

Send a Thank-You Card. The producer and the client want to feel that the project means as much to you as it does to them. Hey, the project might not mean that much to you, but they at least need to know that you appreciate the work. Some people send a card, a little note, or a basket of fruit or flowers. Whatever it is that you decide to do, try to do it within a couple of days after the recording session. Don't get overly sappy with your notes or cards. Keep it simple. It may seem like a little thing to do, but it goes a long way in showing your appreciation.

Yeah, yeah, I gave you a laundry list of things that aren't cool to do and only a couple of things that are great to do, but just these few seemingly minor things are actually pretty major.

Studio Boot Camp

Now that you know how you should conduct yourself in the studio, the next step is understanding how the studio works. Just because you know how to get a splinter from out of the palm of your hand with a straight pin and not draw blood, that doesn't make you a surgeon. Because you know how to hammer some nails into a board in an effort to fix a broken fence, that doesn't make you a carpenter. And just because you know how to sing "Crazy In Love" at the local Karaoke bar you go to every Thursday night, that doesn't make you a studio vocalist. Looking back on the last few chapters, it's easy to see that there is a lot of brain-swelling data to soak in; however, it is crucial for you to have a handle on that information to do any studio job correctly or, as I put it earlier, to stay away from the "A what?" syndrome. Okay, take a quick break, treat yourself to a little something at the local coffee shop (unless you're getting ready to sing today or tomorrow), loosen the belt around your brain, and prepare to have more facts and figures crammed in.

THE RECORDING STUDIO

Now it's time for a quick review. Remember from Chapter 3 that a *studio* is a specially designed, constructed, and/or equipped room or facility used for audio recording. There are many possible configurations of a studio. The variations are largely dependent on its end use; however, the most common setup is that of two adjacent rooms, as in Figures 8.1 and 8.2—basically the studio and the control room.

Figure 8.1

Here is a producer's view from the control room into the studio at Coast Recorders
in San Francisco, California. (Photo by Dan Schmalle, Chris Konovaliv, and Paul Stubblebine.)

Studios, or live rooms, like the one illustrated in Figure 8.3, are typically where guitarists playing through *amplifiers*, keyboardists playing an acoustic piano, or live drummers usually perform during the creation of a sound recording. The *live room* is also the place where vocal magic (hopefully) happens. As a studio singer, you will spend a great deal of time in live rooms, so you should have a solid understanding of the equipment commonly used in these rooms by vocalists to facilitate the recording process. Before I begin dissecting the live room and some of its contents, however, a quick little lesson on the origin of sound seems appropriate.

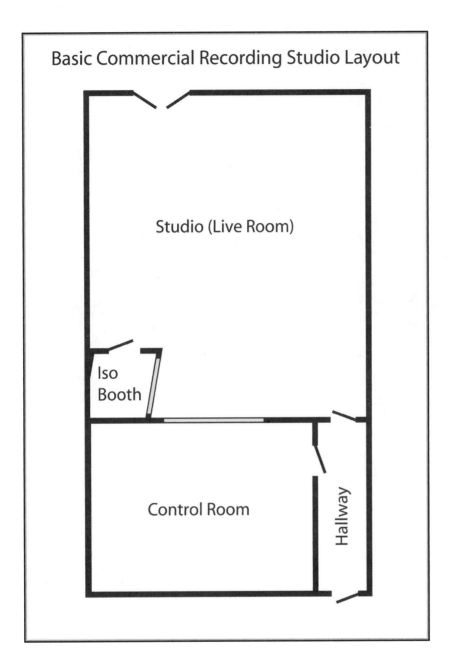

Figure 8.2

This is the basic layout of many commercial studios.

Figure 8.3

Here is a closer look into the studio at Coast Recorders in San Francisco, California.
(Photo by Dan Schmalle, Chris Konovaliv, and Paul Stubblebine.)

 The nomenclature involving the word *studio* can be a bit confusing since an entire recording facility (which includes the control room and the studio—a.k.a. live room) is also called the "studio," "recording studio," "or recording facility." Confused? Not to worry—your understanding will deepen as you see more usages of the word. I promise!

What Is Sound?

Sound starts with vibrating materials. When things vibrate fast enough, they cause the surrounding air particles to push against each other. This creates sound waves that travel through the air. To get a visual illustration, drop a pebble into a body of water. What follows is a ripple effect in the water. Air acts in the same manner. It just takes a higher rate of vibration to get the air to react enough to create the sound waves. When these sound waves, or ripples, reach our ears, the ripples are then converted to nerve impulses that are sent to our brains, thus enabling us to perceive the ripples as sound.

The sound waves we hear are made up of three physical characteristics: *amplitude* (volume—how loud the sound waves are), *frequency* (pitch—the vibration speed of the sound waves), and *harmonic composition* (timbre—the character or quality of the sound waves, which is governed by the makeup of what is creating the sound waves). The combination of these three characteristics allows us to audibly differentiate between, say, a trumpeter loudly playing an A above middle C and a guitarist playing a D-minor chord very softly. In much the same way that our ears pick up the subtleties of sound waves, engineers employ *microphones* as the ears for audio equipment.

Microphones

While creating a beautiful oil painting, a painter will use many different types of tools. Of the many tools at the painter's disposal are a plethora of paintbrushes. The type of effect the painter wants to impart will determine which brush is selected. A #6 flat hog bristle brush may be called for if the painter wants to blend colors over a large area of the canvas. If the painting calls for some fine detailing, a small round sable brush might be employed. Knowledge of the different types of paintbrushes is important if a painter wants to create a quality oil painting. Recording engineers use microphones in a similar manner in an effort to create a quality audio work of art. Just like the painter, the key is for an engineer to learn the different types of microphones, how they differ, how they function, and how that functionality affects how they should be used.

There are three basic types of microphones used in the recording studio: dynamic microphones, ribbon microphones, and condenser microphones.

Dynamic Microphones

Most dynamic microphones are similar in appearance, though there are a few notable exceptions. Figure 8.4 shows one of the more commonly used microphones. Dynamic microphones are built around a thin, round diaphragm, which is the element that senses the incoming sound waves. These microphones are frequently used as broadcast mics. Announcers and radio DJs tend to enjoy the *proximity effect* associated with this type of mic. Of the three types of microphones, dynamic microphones are relatively the least expensive and the most durable, which makes them an excellent choice for live shows, concerts, rehearsals, club performances, and other types of live performances. However, dynamic mics do not find their way into most vocal recording sessions because of their slow response when trying to capture transients (momentary variations in frequency). Many engineers do use them to mic guitar amps, snare drums, and other various instruments.

Ribbon Microphones

Ribbon microphones (see Figure 8.5) use a metal strip of material called a ribbon suspended within a magnetic field as its sound wave-sensitive element. A very dry, meaty sound is usually associated with these mics. Ribbon mics first gained popularity in the early 1940s with jazz singers like Frank Sinatra and Ella Fitzgerald. They are a bit more expensive than dynamic microphones and definitely

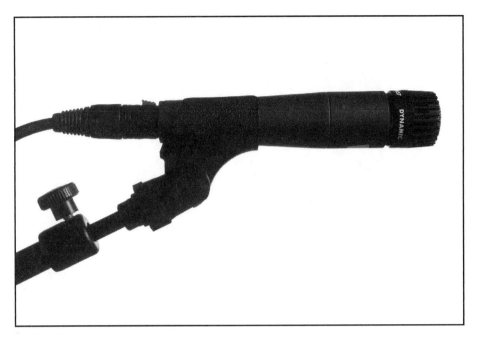

Figure 8.4

The ever-popular Shure SM-57. (Photo by Phil Bray.)

do not have the sturdiness to handle the possible abuses common to live gigs. I find that sometimes ribbon mics can sound a bit dull, though with that being said, there are a few companies such as Beyer and Royer that have been developing brighter sounding ribbon microphones. They are definitely the perfect choice when engineers are trying to get that vintage jazz vocal sound, though because of their beefy sound I have also seen them used on guitar amps and drums.

Condenser Microphones

Like the dynamic microphone, a condenser mic also uses a diaphragm (though slightly larger) as its sound wave-capturing core, but the inner workings are much more complicated. There are actually two types of condenser microphones.

Figure 8.5

A classic RCA ribbon microphone.
(Photo by Phil Bray.)

Solid-State Condenser Microphones are the best at accurately capturing transients. They also have a very wide frequency response, which makes them a great choice as an all-around mic. Over the years, they have become a popular choice for home and project studios because of their brightness and relatively reasonable price.

Historically, these types of microphones have only been utilized in recording studios, radio stations, and any other situation that lends itself to the microphone remaining stationary. With the advances in today's technology, a couple of companies have developed condenser microphones for live performances.

Tube Condenser Microphones, as pictured in Figure 8.6, are my personal favorites for recording vocals. However, this mid-20th century invention is definitely at the top of the food chain, price-wise.

Nowadays, you can find some lower-priced versions that sound quite good by Audio Technica, M-Audio, MXL, Rode, and a host of other companies. Tube condenser mics operate in much the same way as their solid-state counterparts but incorporate a small vacuum tube in their inner workings. The result is a very pleasing "warmth" that I personally love hearing on lead vocals.

Figure 8.6

A favorite among engineers, the Neumann U-87 is shown here with a windscreen. (Photo by Phil Bray.)

As you can see, different microphones can color the sound of vocals in various ways. Sometimes the coloration is desired; other times it isn't. It all depends on the audio "painting" that the engineer is trying to create. When in the studio, be prepared to spend a little time with the engineer having you sing with the music or *a capella,* and possibly into a few different microphones in an effort to find the best mic for recording your voice. A great singer paired with the right microphone can be shear listening magic.

Windscreen

The sensitivity of microphones...Are you getting the feeling that microphones are the divas of the audio world? Anyway, mics are prone to yet another problem, the dreaded "P's," "B's," "T's," "S's," and sometimes "C's." Good singing techniques are the best prevention, although even some of the greatest singers cause booms (Buh – B), pops (Puh – P), and overly extreme sibilance (Sss – S) when singing any of these consonants. *Windscreens* (or *pop filters* as they are also known; see Figures 8.6 and 8.7) help to shield microphones by absorbing the impact of the airbursts caused by these consonants while still allowing the intended sound to get to the microphone.

Figure 8.7

This is a typical vocal session setup with a Neumann U-89 microphone, windscreen, and music stand. (Photo by Phil Bray.)

Gobo

Microphones, especially those as sensitive as condensers, can not only hear the intended sound source, such as a lead vocal, but can also hear the sometimes-unwanted ambience of a large room or a room with a lot of reflective surfaces (reverb, which I'll talk more about later). There are also those occasions when two or more instrumentalists are performing in the studio at the same time. How do you keep a microphone that is listening to one instrument from hearing others? Engineers use devices called *gobos* or *baffles* made of non-reflective materials to minimize unwanted sounds getting into the microphone. Figure 8.3 shows four gobos in use—two to the left of the acoustic piano and two to the right of the organ.

Cue Mix

Background and lead vocalists usually sing to previously recorded *tracks*. The difficulty arises when trying to hear what you are singing while hearing what has already been recorded. The solution is a *cue mix* and *headphones*. A cue mix (also called a headphone mix or cue system) in a recording studio is the headphone link between musicians and vocalists, allowing each to hear his or her own performance in context with those of other musicians, vocalists, and previously recorded tracks.

The cue mix also gives the engineer the ability to selectively change the volume, the tone, or any other elements within the music. That means you can hear the music in a variety of ways. If you are having problems with singing in time, you could have the engineer turn up the drums or other rhythmic instruments. If you are having problems singing in tune, sometimes it's helpful to have the engineer turn up the piano or guitar.

Another great use for the cue mix is the talkback system. This gives the engineer and/or producer the ability to talk to you from the control room while you are in the studio.

Amplifier/Amp: An electronic device used to amplify an incoming audio signal from musical instruments or other sources, which is then coupled to loudspeakers for audible output.

Microphone/Mic: A device that converts sound waves into an electrical signal. Microphones are used in many applications such as telephones, tape recorders, hearing aids, motion picture production, live and recorded audio engineering, radio and television broadcasting, and in computers for recording voice and numerous other computer applications.

Mic (verb): To strategically place a microphone close to the origin of a sound (i.e., a voice or instrument) in order to most faithfully capture, reproduce, transmit, or record the sound.

Proximity Effect: An exaggerated increase in low-frequency response occurring when the sound source is near the microphone. A loss in bass response is experienced as the microphone is moved away from the sound source.

A Cappella: A vocal performance without instrumental accompaniment.

Baffle/Gobo: A moveable shield that is placed around a microphone to keep out unwanted sounds.

Windscreen/Pop Filter: Any device or porous material placed in front of or over a microphone to control the relative intensity of sound waves.

Headphones and Their Proper Use

In New York, I've heard them referred to as "cans" or "headsets." By whatever name, it is essential to understand that, next to the microphone, headphones (like those pictured in Figure 8.8) are one of the most valuable tools of the professional studio vocalist. Their proper use is a vital aid in delivering a great performance in a recording session.

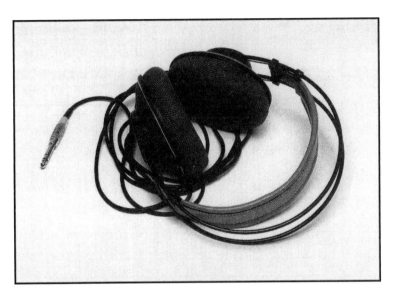

Figure 8.8

A typical set of headphones used in the studio.

Now when I said "next to the microphone," I meant that figuratively of course, for here is your first and most important lesson about headphones: Never stand close to a live microphone when putting on or taking off headphones. Doing so could cause one of the most horrendous sounds known to man: *feedback*. (If you'd like to hear a tame version of feedback, see ws_08-01.mp3 on the companion Web site.) Believe me, you do not want this sound to occur anywhere near your ears. Aside from the annoyance factor, the sound can cause damage not only to your ears, but to the ears of everyone else wearing headphones and anyone listening in the control room. Always take a couple of steps back from the microphone before donning or removing headphones. Also, once you've taken them off, never set the headphones down near a live microphone or hang them on the microphone stand.

While in the studio, headphones are usually the only way that you can hear the accompanying music you need to sing with; however, the mistake made by most inexperienced singers is fully covering their ears when wearing them. Most singers are used to hearing the sound of their voice in an ambient space, be it in a classroom, in the backyard, on stage, at church, in the bathroom shower, and so on.

(Although, with the proliferation of the iPod, it seems like people are wearing headsets all of the time.) As an experiment, cup your hands and place them over your ears, completely covering them. Then sing anything you like. What you hear is the sound of your voice inside of your head. This is also what happens when the headphones are worn completely over your ears. The problem is that it becomes very difficult, if not impossible, to judge things like whether you are singing *sharp* or *flat*, or how loud or soft you are singing. There are three ways to wear headphones that aid in a singer's need to hear their voice in the room.

One of the most common ways of wearing headphones is with one side off and muffled against the back of your head, while the other side covers the other ear completely, as shown in Figure 8.9. Which ear you choose to cover I suppose is dependent on whether you are left- or right-brained. Seriously, experiment with both ways and you'll quickly find out which way is the most comfortable. Take care to make sure that you dampen the sound coming from the side that is not on your ear to prevent feedback or *bleed*.

Figure 8.9

The best way to use headphones is with one side off the ear and muffled against the back of the head. (Photo by Phil Bray.)

Track: In recording, a discrete or distinguishable strip or path along the length of a magnetic tape (or a segment of a computer hard drive), on which data or sound can be recorded and played back separately from the other tracks on the tape (or computer hard drive).

Headphones/Cans/Headset/Earphones: A binaural audio output device, usually fitted to the ears with a band passing over the head.

Feedback: An unwanted audio noise caused by the return of sound from headphones through the input source of the microphone.

Talkback: A communication device that links performers in the studio with a producer or engineer in the control room.

Sharp: To sing above the proper or indicated pitch.

Flat: To sing below the proper or indicated pitch.

Bleed: In recording, leakage occurring when sound emanating from one source (e.g., a headset, instrument, or amplifier) is picked up by a microphone placed to pick up sound from another source.

The second way, as shown in Figure 8.10, is to have one side partially off one ear just enough to still hear in the room, while still being able to totally hear through the side of the headphones that completely covers the other ear. I like this method because I'm getting the music to both ears while still hearing myself in the room. You have to be extra careful with this method, however, as you can cause a bit of bleed.

The third way is to have both sides partially off your ears. I mostly use this method when I'm singing background vocals with a group of other singers so that I can clearly hear the other vocalists in the room as well as how their voices interact with mine. Of course, this method has a double chance of causing bleed, so you really have to make sure that the headphones are snug to your head.

Figure 8.10

Another great way to wear headphones is with one side half off of the ear. (Photo by Phil Bray.)

Speaking of snug, make sure that the headphones fit comfortably. They shouldn't be too tight, especially since you normally will have to wear them for a while. Too loose is also no good. Who wants to be wrestling with a set of headphones that are constantly falling off? Don't be afraid to ask for another set of headphones if the ones you have aren't feeling right. On another note, I usually carry my own set of headphones to recording sessions. I'll first try out the ones at the studio, and then if those don't work out, I break out my own set.

Another reason for bringing my own headphones is that I am familiar with how they sound. From studio to studio, you will encounter a variety of headphones. Some will sound great, while others will leave much to desire. Headphones aren't where studio owners spend the big bucks. Of all the equipment in the studio, headphones are the most abused. They will constantly be dropped, stepped on, and mishandled. So studio owners usually opt to buy mid-priced headphones—something that will do the trick, yet won't cost a lot of money to replace.

Circumaural closed-back headphones like the ones shown in Figures 8.9 and 8.10 are the best for studio use. They fully cover your ears (unless you wear them as suggested earlier) and are designed to minimize bleed and feedback. They are also the most comfortable to wear. Noise-canceling headphones are also circumaural and closed-back in design. They are good at shielding out surrounding sounds such as air conditioning, the low-end rumble of a train, and so on. However, engineers usually record vocalists in rooms that are sound proof, so that type of headphone would be useless to vocalists; however, they would be great for drummers trying to play to a pre-recorded track. Noise-canceling headphones are usually expensive, making them quite rare in a recording studio. Circumaural open-back headphones are comfortable to wear, too, but aren't as suitable for studio use. Some club DJs use them while mixing because they can listen to music without external sounds being blocked out. However, the same design also allows sound to leak from those headphones. *Supra-aural* headphones such as the ear-buds that come with iPods and other mp3 players should not be used in the studio. The sound quality is insufficient for studio use, and they tend to bleed a lot.

Circumaural: The headphone pads go around your ears.

Supra-aural: The headphone pads rest on your ears.

AKG and Sony make most of the headphones that I have seen used in studios, but there is no standard brand. As for the headphones that I like to carry around, I have an affinity for the Sony MDR-V6. The high end is crystal clear and the bass is punchy. Plus, there is the added bonus of being able to fold them down and store them in a leather carrying case that comes with the headphones.

Headphone Amplifier

In many home or project studios this is a luxury, but in the majority of commercial studios you will encounter a headphone amp or a junction box of some type that is used to power and control the volume of headphones. Some will have knobs enabling you to turn individual instruments up and down, while others will only allow control of the overall volume. Care should be taken in how loud you choose to have your headphones, as they can cause bleed. (For an example, see ws_08-02.mp3 on the companion Web site.) Over a period of time, too much volume in your headphones will cause ear fatigue. Once your ears get tired, it becomes difficult to judge your pitch and volume. When that starts to happen, it's time to take a break!

Music Stand

I'm sure that you know what a music stand is, but take another look at Figure 8.7 just in case. Some music stands are made of materials that can be very reflective, so don't be surprised if the engineer puts some sort of sound-absorbing cloth or other non-reflective material over the face of the music stand. No, it's not for aesthetics. Even though the cloth may match the room, its actual purpose is to prevent the sound of a singer's voice from bouncing off of the music stand back into the microphone.

Aside from holding the lyrics, a lead sheet, or some sort of vocal chart, I like to use a music stand for what I call "utility items." For example, I take a pencil into the studio. Change is a constant thing during recording, and a pencil will help you roll with those changes. Bring a bottle of water (preferably at room temperature). I also like to bring a tin of mints to background vocal sessions in an effort to not make the session any harder than it has to be.

Vocal Booth

Another room that you will encounter in most commercial studios is a vocal booth. This is a smaller room built inside of the studio.

Other names for this room are "isolation booth" or "iso booth" because of its use to isolate things like a loud guitar amp or a lead vocalist. Check out the view from within an iso booth in Figure 8.11.

Figure 8.11

Here is a singer's view from inside the iso booth at Yonas Media East in New York. (Photo by Daniel Norton.)

THE CONTROL ROOM

The second most important room in a studio facility (aside from the bathroom) is the control room. Recall from Chapter 7 that the control room is a room separated from a studio (live room), which contains the mixing console and recording equipment, and in which the engineer and/or producer oversees the recording of a performance. There is some key equipment for vocalists to take note of in this room as well.

Mixing Console Basics

The mixer (or board, or mixing console) is an electronic device used by recording engineers to combine several audio signals onto one or more tracks on a segment of a computer hard drive (or a magnetic tape). See Figure 8.12 for an example of a mixing console. The 21st century has brought about computer-based digital audio workstations (DAWs) such as ProTools, Digital Performer, and Logic Audio, to name a few. These programs have not only replaced the need for recording tape, but also include built-in digital versions of mixing consoles (see Figure 8.13).

Figure 8.12

The mixing console at Infinite Studios in Alameda, California. (Photo by Phil Bray.)

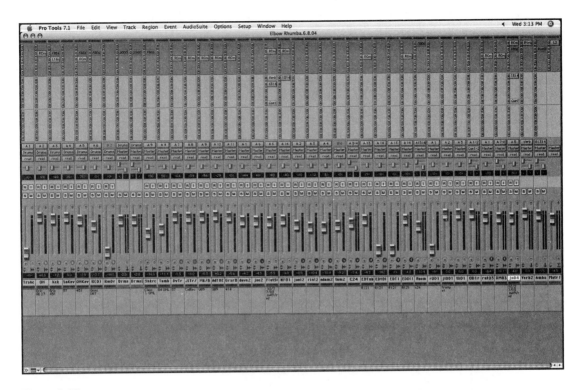

Figure 8.13

A screenshot of a ProTools-based recording session. (Screenshot provided by Lu Miranda.)

As I said, I'm not trying to train you to be a recording engineer, but there are some basic things that you should know about mixing consoles. Besides being the conduit through which audio is recorded to a hard drive or tape, mixers are also used to play back and *mix* the audio that has been recorded. There are a few parts of the mixer that are very helpful for a singer to know. Understanding what these mixer functions are will go a long way toward the communication between the singer and the producer or engineer.

When looking at a mixer, the first thing usually said by the novice is, "Whoa! That's a whole lot of knobs!" Don't panic. I'll try to break things down a bit. The channels on a mixer can be used both to record sound to and play back sound from a hard drive or tape recorder. If you look at the mixer closely, you will notice that each channel has a number. Here's the trick to a mixer: If you learn one channel column, then you basically know most of the mixer, so for the purpose of this section, all of my comments will refer to channel one. As I explain some of the parts of the mixer, please refer to Figure 8.14. I will "K.I.S." (Keep It Simple) as much as possible.

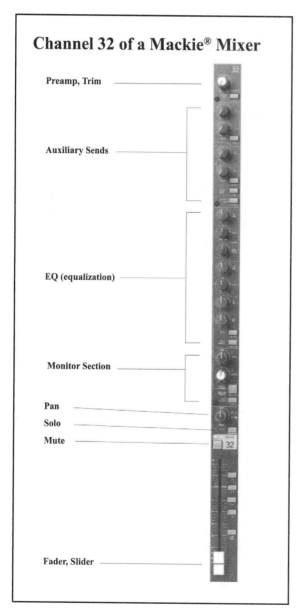

Channel 32 of a Mackie® Mixer

Preamp, Trim

Auxiliary Sends

EQ (equalization)

Monitor Section

Pan
Solo
Mute

Fader, Slider

Figure 8.14

One channel pulled from a Mackie 32•8 Mixer.

As diverse as microphones are, so too are mixing consoles. Though all mixers will have the same basic controls, different mixers will have the configurations of these controls set up slightly differently. Some will have less detailing in the controls, while others will have more.

Inputs and Preamp

Starting from the parts of the mixer that generally are not seen are a couple of different types of inputs. These inputs are how the sounds generated from guitars, microphones, synthesizers, etc. are plugged into the mixer.

Most microphones and some electronic instruments like guitar, do not have amplification adequate enough for recording. There has to be something that can bring their volume up loud enough to be correctly recorded. Looking at Figure 8.14, you can see that this particular mixer accomplishes this with a built-in *preamp*, also called trim. Some engineers prefer to use external preamp devices, especially when it comes to vocals.

Auxiliary Sends

Next in line is a set of Auxiliary Sends. These sends route whatever is on this channel to effects such as digital delays or reverbs. This board has the capability to route the source sound to at least six different effects (two of the knobs have double duty). I'll talk about effects a bit later.

Mix: To combine and blend two or more separately recorded tracks into one or two equalized tracks.

Preamp/Preamplifier: An electronic device commonly used to amplify microphones, electronic instruments, and other electronic devices.

EQ

The Equalization (EQ) section is next. EQ is a way of controlling and editing sound wave frequencies. If you take a look at a home audio amplifier, you will see two or three knobs or levers labeled Treble, Mid-Range, and Bass. When you turn the Treble knob up or down, you increase or decrease an entire range of high-end frequencies. Likewise, when you turn up or down the Mid-Range knob, the same thing happens to a host of mid-range frequencies. And so it goes with the bass knob. This is a simplified version of EQ. The EQ section of the mixer can not only boost or decrease entire ranges of frequencies, but also has the ability to dial in a specific frequency in which to edit. On the mixer in Figure 8.14, there are a set of controls for the upper mid-range frequencies, for the lower mid-range frequencies, for overall treble, and for overall bass. Many other mixers such as the one pictured in Figure 8.12 can have a more detailed EQ section.

Monitor Section

This part of the mixer is where the cue mix is put together. Most details were covered earlier in the section "Cue Mix."

Pan

The Pan control gives the engineer the ability to place a sound signal from left to right, right to left, or to the center of a stereo image. Notice that the Monitor section has a Pan knob as well. This is an especially useful tool when you are *multi-tracking* vocals. You can have the engineer pan all of the recorded vocal tracks to one side of the headphones while listening to the track you are currently singing on the other side. This makes it easy to audibly distinguish what you are currently singing from your earlier recorded vocal tracks.

Solo

Pressing the Solo button turns other channels off and plays this channel only. Its use to a singer becomes obvious if that singer is trying to learn a previously recorded vocal part, yet the part is hard to hear because of the accompanying music tracks. You can also put a few channels in solo at the same time.

Mute

Pressing the Mute button turns the channel off. Many times when doing lead or background vocals you might need the engineer to turn off tracks that make it difficult to hear the pitch or rhythm correctly. Maybe it's just that there are too many music or vocal tracks that are distracting. The answer is simple: "Mute." (Don't you wish some people came with this button?)

Fader

Lastly, the Fader (or Slider) is a control device on a mixer by which sound levels are changed.

 Multi-tracking: Recording additional tracks electronically or mechanically, containing the same material as recorded on the original track.

There are many more knobs, buttons, and switches that I haven't touched upon. That's only because the goal here is for you to be able to communicate your needs when trying to record vocals, and the controls I've discussed are the ones that will best facilitate that goal. Whenever you have an opportunity, please experiment with these controls to get a better understanding of their functions.

Effects

While listening to CDs of different recording artists, you will encounter a great many different types of effects used on vocals. Some are used just to add a bit of the ambience that we are used to hearing with a voice, some are used to correct or cover up deficiencies in vocal performances, while others are used simply to provide a unique musical statement. No matter what the use, a vocalist should at least understand some of the more basic effects used on voices.

Reverb

If you stand in the entryway of an office building and speak very loud, you'll not only hear the sound of your voice, but the sound of your voice reflecting off of surfaces such as windows, drywall, wood doors, tiled floors, or any other solid surfaces present. Our ears pick up these reflective sounds, and we perceive this as room ambience (reverb). There are electronic devices used in recording, playback, and mixing to simulate natural reverb effects. In the DAWs realm there are digital versions of these devices called plugins. To hear a few reverb effects, check out ws_08-03.mp3 on the companion Web site.

Many singers like to hear reverb on their voice in the headphones as they are recording. Be careful with this. Too much reverb can hinder your ability to hear the pitch correctly and can throw your sense of timing off a bit.

Compressor–Limiter

Compressor–limiters are signal processing devices used in recording and mixing to limit the range of dynamic responses from sound sources in order to present a more even, less erratic volume level. One of the most dynamic instruments is the human voice. At a moment's notice a singer can go from very soft to ultra loud. When trying to capture a vocalist's performance, it sometimes becomes necessary to control that dynamic range. Compressors or limiters used sparingly will accomplish this. They both can be set to limit the volume of incoming audio to a predetermined level. So, if the dynamics of the incoming audio is greater than this set level, the volume is reduced. On the other hand, the compressor can be set such that if the incoming audio is too soft, the volume will be raised. The problem with both of these tools comes with excessive use. Overuse will result in a vocal track sounding squeezed or strained.

Digital Delay

Digital delay is a digital signal-processing (DSP) device used in recording and mixing to electronically add or adjust the delay of an audio signal to give the perception of "slap echo" or doubling. To the layperson this is, this is, this is, called, called, called, echo, echo, echo. Digital delay can also be used as an effect that goes with the beat, or it can be used to make a singer sound as if his vocal track has been doubled. Listen to ws_08-04.mp3 on the companion Web site.

Autotune

Autotune is an effect that was made famous in the DAW's world. Its claim to fame is its ability to tune a vocalist's tracks. However, I've seen many vocalists come into the studio, sing a few tracks, and then say to the producer, "I like that track, but it's out of tune. Can you just send it through Autotune?" Come on! How lazy can they be? Maybe it's just me, but I've always felt that part of being a great singer is having the pride to want to sing in tune—to want to have a great sense of rhythm, and to have a need to relish in singing with feeling. Well, alright, I will concede that every now and then there is a justification for using this tool. I've been in situations where I have sung passages that had great feeling, but there was one note sung out of tune. Rather than risk the passage possibly having a different feel after trying to sing it again, the producer opted to just tune that one note. My point is that it should be used as a tool and not as a crutch. There is no substitute for first-rate singing.

The recording studio can be a formidable, intimidating place, or it can feel like home. It is your responsibility to learn what is necessary to make it the latter. See if you can hook up with local engineers who may be willing to help you learn more about the studio and its ancillary equipment. Remember, as I said earlier in the book, "A closed mouth never gets fed."

Lead Vocals

The music world has gone through scores of technical changes. Throughout the years, I have seen transformations from recording on 2-inch tape, to ADAT, to the current flavor of the times, computer-based digital audio workstations (DAWs). I have witnessed the proliferation and growth of sequencers and samplers. Even the replacement of vinyl 45s and CD singles with the 21st-century mp3s has transpired during my lifetime. With all of the technological advances happening every day, there are still a few things that the computer cannot do, and one of those is the emulation of the lead singer. Sure, you can sample vocal parts and use them in varied but limited situations. If a singer has a bit of a timing problem, you can shift that audio around to fix the problem. Nowadays, the computer can even correct minor deficiencies in a singer's pitch with tools like AutoTune (check out ws_09-01.mp3 on the companion Web site). Still, it can't yet generate all of the subtle nuances of a singer's voice. Things like tone, style, and feeling are attributes that are still privy to being human. Who knows what the future holds, but for now the role of a lead vocalist means being the featured *person*. The vocalist has the responsibility to bring to the table all of the qualities associated with lead vocals. Whether it's singing in front of a band, being a recording artist, or singing for commercial sessions, it means being well acquainted with how your voice functions and how to take care of it.

Doonesbury copyright 1986 G. B. Trudeau.
Reprinted with permission of Universal Press Syndicate. All rights reserved.

VOICE PRODUCTION

Instruments of all types use different ways to create sound waves (as discussed in Chapter 8). A clarinet has a reed that vibrates against a mouthpiece. A guitar has strings that vibrate when they are strummed, and a trumpet has the musician's lips vibrating together in a metal mouthpiece. Of all the instruments in the world, however, none is more beautiful or delicate than the human voice.

We all have what's called a voice box (or, for you techies out there, a larynx), which is a cylinder-shaped structure comprised of cartilage. Anchored to this cartilage are vocal cords (a.k.a. vocal folds) that visually resemble small lips and have the ability to react to the passage of air from our lungs. (See ws_09-02.mp4 on the companion Web site for a video example of vocal cords at work.)

We have the innate ability to make our vocal cords vibrate at different rates of speed, thus giving us the ability to talk and sing a range of different notes. The actual range is defined by how large or small an individual's vocal chords are. Everyone's vocal cords are different in size, which explains why some people can sing higher or lower than others.

TECHNIQUES

While trying to perform your best behind the microphone, a great many things can be distracting. However, the only thing you should be thinking about is how to emote the feelings called for by the song. To successfully accomplish this requires some expertise with a few technical and preparation skills.

Choosing the Right Key

Regardless of whether the recording project that you'll be working on is for yourself or for a client, long before you start to record you need to consider the *key* in which you will sing. Most singers are not blessed with a five-*octave* vocal range. Not every set of men or women has the same vocal ranges. If you compare Stevie Wonder to Marc Anthony or Kelly Clarkson to Beyoncé, you can quickly hear the obvious: differences in style, tone, and techniques. Less obvious is the fact that they have different vocal ranges. Each of these singers spends a good bit of time making sure that the songs that they sing are recorded in the keys that best compliment their style, tone, and range. Choosing the right keys in which to sing your songs could be the very thing that makes or breaks how well you perform. There is one song that illustrates this point better than any other song that I can think of: "The Star Spangled Banner" (see Figure 9.1). I don't have enough fingers or toes to count how many times I've seen a singer go down the tubes singing this song in the wrong key. Does "And the rockets red glare" sound familiar? If not, check out the file ws_09-03.mp3 on the companion Web site.

Figure 9.1

"The Star Spangled Banner" is a song to live or die by depending on the key you sing it in.

The human singing voice is often categorized into four basic ranges: soprano, alto, tenor, and bass. Figure 9.2 shows these different singing ranges. It is important to know that there are also sub-categories of vocal ranges such as mezzo soprano, contralto, baritone, and so on. Of lesser importance is whether your voice adheres strictly to any of these ranges. Use these ranges merely as a loose guide to aid in choosing the right keys for songs you perform.

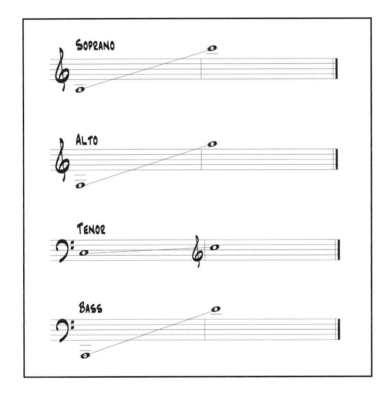

Figure 9.2

The basic singing ranges.

When selecting the key for a song, make sure that you have an idea of the vocal range covered by the song. If you don't play an instrument like the piano or guitar, then the next step would be to hook up with an *accompanist* (preferably someone who has the ability to *transpose* the song). Have that person play the song in the original key and sing along to see how that key fits with your voice.

Don't worry about trying to do the whole song. Just pick out the sections of the song that contain the highest and lowest notes. Go over just those parts. If you find that you are straining to hit the higher notes, keep lowering the key until you find a key where it is both comfortable for you to sing and it helps you exhibit the best parts of your voice. Do the reverse if you find that the lower notes of the song are either hard to sing or you just don't sound good singing in that range.

Key: The interrelationship between tones based on the seven tones of a major or minor scale and centered around a fundamental tone, usually called the tonic.

Octave: A tone that is eight full tones above or below another given tone.

Accompanist: A performer, such as a pianist, who plays an accompaniment.

Transpose: Playing the song in a key different from the original key.

If you have a synthesizer that includes a piano sound, I have an easy way for you to work on finding keys. Most synthesizers have within their global editing section the ability to change the overall key of the synthesizer just by pressing a button or moving a lever. That way you only have to know how to play the song in one key and then use the controls on the synthesizer to change keys. You can also use a karaoke-style player if you have the music on a CD. These players usually have the ability to temporarily change the key of the song during playback.

When you get called for a lead vocal session, see if the producer is willing to give you a copy of the song, with maybe a *reference vocal* or at least with an instrument playing the melody to help you determine if the key is good for your voice. If it is not, ask if the producer can change the key before you go in for the session. Sometimes the producer may not be able to make that key change. If that is the case, and you know that the song is in a key that makes it impossible to sing correctly, your best bet is to politely decline doing the session. If there is another vocalist you can recommend, do so. You are much better off not embarrassing yourself by trying to sing a song that is out of your vocal range. There have been plenty of times when I have told producers, "I don't think that I am right for this song. I'd like to recommend someone else rather than waste costly studio time." Knowledgeable and experienced producers will respect you for that decision. In many cases, I've actually ended up getting more work from those particular producers because I was so honest and upfront.

A quick word on recommendations: Before recommending anyone, you need to know that they can really handle the job. You want to know as much about their personality, dependability, and work ethic as possible. The reason being, as the dictionary says, is that you are putting forward someone with approval as being suitable for a particular purpose or role. If you recommend someone who can't handle the gig, is late, or is unprepared, it not only reflects badly on that person but, unfortunately, on *you* too!! Worse yet, the next time you recommend someone to that client, that client will surely be looking at you cross-eyed.

Do Your Homework

Producers or clients will sometimes send you a CD or mp3 and a *lyric sheet* (see Figure 9.3) or *lead sheet* (see Figure 9.1) to study days before a recording session. Please do your homework. If you want to do your best in the studio, preparedness is essential. Being prepared also shows respect for your client's project. The client is spending money on an engineer, the studio, and whatever else...oh yeah, and you! All of which are usually on an hourly rate. You're doing yourself a great disservice, as well as wasting your client's time and money, when you show up unprepared.

I Lose Sleep Over You

(Claytoven Richardson - Yvonne Bennett)

Hot summer night
Curtains blowing in the wind
I tried to call
but you were out again
I toss and turn
My body yearns
to have your love all over me
but all I have
is fantasies

I want you in my bed
beside me
I lie alone instead
Lonely me

Chorus:
I lose sleep over you
I lose sleep
I lose sleep over you
I lose sleep

Can't wait to taste
the sweetness of your love
Like fine champagne
I get too little of
The hours pass
This feeling lasts
My body heat won't let me rest
Let's face it, girl
your love's the best

I want you in my bed
beside me
I lie alone instead
Lonely me

Chorus:

Figure 9.3

An example of a lyric sheet.

Reference Vocal: A vocal frequently used solely for demonstration.

Lyric Sheet: A sheet that contains the words to a song (see Figure 9.3).

Lead Sheet: Musical notation containing a song's melody line, together with lyrics and chord symbols, but not fully orchestrated (see Figure 9.1).

Memorization

A part of being prepared is memorizing the lyrics to the song whenever you can. You want to spend the majority of your time behind the microphone thinking about how to convey the emotions in a song as opposed to trying to keep track of where you are on a lyric sheet. It's just another distraction you want to eliminate. It's okay to have the lyric sheet with you on a music stand in the studio just in case of an occasional memory lapse or if the producer wants to *punch in* or *punch out* at a particular spot in the song.

Punch In: The act of putting a recording device into the record mode in order to insert or overdub new or additional material.

Punch Out: The act of taking a recording device out of the record mode.

I was in my home office going through an incredibly ironic bout of writer's block while trying to write this section on memorization. As I sat at my desk struggling to put my thoughts together, my 5-year-old daughter interrupted me by playing her CD player very loudly in her room. I go to her room and I am about to tell her to quiet down when I see she is sitting on the floor with her back to me.

She is so busy that she doesn't notice that I am standing in her doorway. I listen to her singing the melody to the last part of the song she is playing. Then the song ends and she immediately starts it over. I notice that all the while the music is playing she is singing the melody and every now and then she puts in a couple of lyrics that she knows. The song gets to the end again and she starts it over again. This time when the music gets to a certain point, she quickly winds it back to a particular spot. She listens and then winds it back to that spot again. Then she sings the lyrics she just heard. The process continues until she gets through the whole song. Then she takes the player back to the beginning again and sings the melody and lyrics all the way through. There was my 5-year-old doing my memorization technique. I guess she had been watching me more than I thought during my practices for my gigs. At least that's what I would like to think. Anyway, try this technique for yourself. It really does work.

Singing in Tune (Pitch)

One of the hardest things for a vocalist to do in the studio is sing *in tune*. There are usually two reasons for the difficulty: not enough voice training or the improper use of headphones. From time to time, even the best vocalist will have a couple of pitch problems during some sessions. Unfortunately, a vocalist doesn't come with tuning pegs like a guitar or other ways to tune such as with a clarinet or trumpet. However, while doing sessions and gigs with musicians, I did get a great idea from watching guitarists tune their instruments. Guitar tuners are small and inexpensive gadgets that guitarists use. As you play the instrument, it figures out what note you are playing and then indicates by way of a small meter whether the note is in tune. I figured, why not try it out on vocals? So I went to the local music store and bought a chromatic guitar tuner, similar to the one pictured in Figure 9.4. It was a great investment, considering that it had a built-in microphone and cost only around $85. I used it by first playing a note on a keyboard, and then, while trying to match the note I just played, I would sing into the tuner while watching the meter. Visually seeing where your pitch is can be a very helpful tool. Eventually, with some practice, my pitch improved incredibly. Try this technique for yourself and, with a little practice, you too will eventually find that even without the tuner you will start to hear when you are a bit off in pitch.

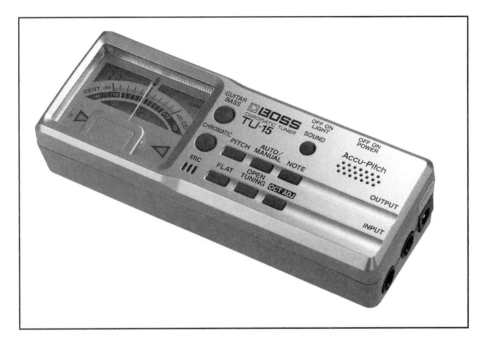

Figure 9.4

A Boss chromatic guitar tuner, one of many types of tuners.

 In Tune: To sing the proper or indicated pitch.

Improving Timing

Another problem common to many vocalists is singing out of time, or as most producers say, singing off beat. I have spent many years with private instructors working with me as both a singer and instrumentalist. After a while, I started to notice a pattern. All of my lessons as an instrumentalist were conducted while a *metronome* was keeping the beat. Take a quick look at the Oxford American definition of a metronome: "A device used by musicians that marks time at a selected rate by giving a regular tick." Notice the mention of musicians and not vocalists. That's not right!

 Metronome: A device used by musicians *and vocalists* that marks time at a selected rate by emitting a regular click sound.

All of my lessons as a vocalist were with an accompanist or *a cappella*, and definitely sans metronome. After talking with a lot of singers, I found that experience to be quite commonplace. As an experiment, I started using a metronome when practicing all of my vocal exercises and songs. Within a couple of weeks, I noticed that my timing during vocal sessions was consistently improving. Today, producers and other singers tell me that I have the timing of a drummer. Try using a metronome during your lessons and when you practice. You will be surprisingly pleased at the results.

Style

There is a tendency in the music business for everything to be categorized, especially when it comes to singers. One of my most hated phrases to hear is, "Oh, you sound like...." You want to be different—something special. The problem is that difference is a very difficult thing for the listening audience to accept, although most successful singers go against the grain with regards to style. No matter what the song, the great singers sing them *their* way, while sometimes unconsciously rebuking the status quo. I am of the opinion that it is better to be a trendsetter than a trend follower, so a lot of time and consideration should be put into your "original" singing style.

Style consists of things like the way you use your vibrato, the way you pronounce certain words, whether you sing edgy or smoothly, the tone of your voice, and a number of other things that define the originality of your voice. One of the hardest things for a new singer to do is to accept what makes their voice different. In my earlier years, I spent a good deal of my time trying to sound like Stevie Wonder. After an unsuccessful year at that attempt, a producer finally said to me, "Claytoven, why don't you sing the way your voice wants you to? I like when you do that better than what you are trying to do." You will go your entire career with people trying to compare your singing with that of other established singers. Fortune doesn't always strike, with someone being honest and talking to you about your being reluctant to do *your* thing. But, wait a minute, that's what I'm telling you now! Spend some time truly listening to how you sing. Figure out and embrace what makes you different from other singers. Along with spending time to develop your basic singing techniques, do not be afraid to take time to work on enhancing the originality of your voice.

There was a great vocalist for whom I once produced a record. Her name was Tammi, a 17-year-old phenom with a wonderfully sultry voice that was real appealing to the record company to which she was signed. After the release of her first single, she spent a lot of time singing with me on a great deal of recording sessions. About a year passed, and her single was doing quite well. The success prompted the record company to ask her to do a full album. When we were finished with a couple of new songs, I turned them in to the record company just to get a take on what they thought. The A&R director called me a few days later expressing his disappointment at how Tammi sounded. I was told that there was something different about her voice. Though the A&R director couldn't explain exactly what the problem was, he just didn't like the change. After a few more weeks of working with Tammi, I finally realized what was happening. Over the span of a year, she had systematically changed the speed of her vibrato in an effort to sing the way her friends thought she should. The change was so gradual that I hadn't noticed. We finally corrected the problem and once again she was the darling of the record company.

It's the same thing when you get hired for a recording session. When a producer hires you, it is usually based on having heard you at a gig, on a demo, on a project on which you participated, or possibly at someone else's recording session. Many singers make the mistake of changing the way that they sing in an effort to sound the way that they think the producer wants. There is an old Billy Joel song that starts off with, "Don't go changing, to try and please me, you never let me down before." Keep in mind that clients hire you based on what they have heard you do (hopefully), not based on how they can change what you do.

Attitude

In 1985, I was a part of a band called Makoto that was briefly signed to Qwest Records. It was during the recording of the one and only album that we did for that label that I had the honor of meeting one of the greatest producers of all times, Quincy Jones. While in the middle of weeks of recording, he came by one day to check on our progress. As he sat and listened to some of the songs that we were working on, he uttered one of the most profound statements that I have ever heard: "A singer is only as good as the song." I didn't realize it then, but that was the quote of the century! At the time, it was a serious ego buster for me since I was one of the lead singers, yet he was and still is totally right. There are a lot of incredible singers everywhere, but without a hit song, all of someone's vocal acrobatics mean nothing. The song is king, and as a vocalist your job is to capture and effectively convey the emotions of the song. If you don't do that, you're just singing words. To effectively capture the right mood, you have to understand what the song is talking about. You have to be capable of emoting the feelings that the writer is trying to convey. Before you make your first attempt at trying to sing the song, read through the lyrics a few times. Figure out what the story is all about. Then try to think of a similar experience in your life that can help you get in touch with the writer's emotions. Bring those emotions with you to use in the studio. Take a little time before you start to record the song to get into the mood. Don't be afraid to put that attitude into your singing. To paraphrase another great producer, Narada Michael Walden if the song is supposed to make you cry, and if when you sing you don't cry, then why should I?

Microphone Techniques

Okay, here I go again talking about that audio diva, the microphone. Below are a couple of quick things to remember and practice for your grand entrance into the world of the studio.

Positioning

Where you stand in reference to the microphone makes a big difference in how the microphone hears you and how the recording of your voice sounds. Start off standing about six inches away from the microphone. The engineer will sometimes have you sing the song *a cappella* and often *cold* just to get an idea of your volume. If the engineer wants you to stand in a different position, you will be asked to move a bit closer or to step back. On ballads, or if you tend to sing a bit soft, the engineer may have you stand very close to the microphone. If you are singing a rock song or you are a belter, the engineer may have you stand as much as a foot and a half from the microphone. Once the perfect position has been established, make sure that you remember exactly where you are standing. There are times when you will need to go into the control room to listen to your performances, or you may just need to take a restroom break. When you get back in front of the microphone, the engineer will definitely not appreciate having to reestablish your positioning. One of my favorite tricks is to put down some tape marking the position of my feet. For a while, I even brought my own quick-release painter's tape (drafting tape works great, too) to the recording sessions until I became an expert at remembering my mic positioning.

Take note of how loud you speak as opposed to how loud you sing. If you tend to talk much louder than you sing, keep that in mind. For obvious reasons, you will either want to step back from the mic when you speak or try to talk a bit softer.

The reason for using painter's or drafting tape is that it can stick to surfaces without causing damage when it is removed. Don't use tapes with strong glues, such as gaffer's tape or electrical tape.

Cold: A quick, unrehearsed run-through of a performance.

T's, S's, P's, and B's

I covered the windscreen part of dealing with problematic consonants in the last chapter; however, there is more you can do to cut down on this problem. The trick is to practice trying to soften the sound of these consonants when pronouncing them. Also, try taking a speaking class that will help with your enunciation of these and other consonants and vowel sounds.

Mic Adjustments

There are times when you may need the microphone to be adjusted. Maybe it's a little too high for you, or maybe it's set up in a way that feels awkward. If so, ask the engineer to make the adjustments. Never try to do it yourself for two reasons:

First, you have no way of knowing if the mic is hot and how loud it may be. Your trying to make adjustments to the mic may cause very loud sounds in the control room, which could possibly damage a speaker or, worse, cause injury to someone's ears.

Second, you could accidentally cause damage to the microphone itself. Man, you don't want the bill associated with the replacement of an expensive condenser mic!

Whenever you ask to have adjustments made to the microphone or cue mix, temporarily remove your headphones, just in case. Accidents sometimes happen. Why take a chance on a sudden volume increase, feedback, or any other noise that could possibly injure your ears while wearing headphones?

Practice, Practice, Practice

Although everyone has the innate ability to sing, being able to sing songs in a way that is both musical and pleasing to others is a skill. The top vocalists are those who can come into the studio and effortlessly wow a producer. Speed and accuracy are major parts of that wow factor. A vocalist who can flawlessly combine pitch, execution, style, and attitude and walk away leaving the producer with great vocal tracks, while also saving the producer money in studio time, is more valuable than gold. These attributes come from tons of dedicated practice.

Another aid in the speed department is coming to sessions with your voice ready to go. A quarterback or pitcher doesn't come out of the locker room, get immediately in the game, and start throwing 60-yard passes or 90-mph fast balls without first warming up with a few practice throws. They wouldn't be able to perform at their best. There is also a higher risk of an injury. Treat your voice the same way as these pro athletes treat their arms, by warming up before you get into any heavy singing. There are sessions where the producer must adhere to a deadline, and in those cases walking in the door ready to sing becomes a major time-saver. While on the way to most of my recording sessions, drivers on the highway get a pretty crazy-looking show watching me do vocal exercises in my car.

The more studio experience you get under your belt, the better you become; however, in the beginning, you may not be in the studio every day or as frequently as you would like. Try putting together a small computer DAW system at home. There are many low-cost audio programs to choose from (e.g., ProTools LE, Digital Performer, Logic Audio, etc.). Not only will a DAW give you a forum in which to practice, it will also go a long way toward your understanding of studio equipment.

Invest in a good vocal coach. You may have to go through a few different coaches before you find the one with whom you feel comfortable. Plan on having a vocal coach of some kind throughout your entire career. Great singers continually try to put themselves in the position of learning new things to broaden their singing prowess. I once heard songwriter–singer Lionel Ritchie say, "Once you think you know everything, that's when your career starts to end."

VOICE CARE

When a string breaks on a violin, it can be replaced with a new one. Most saxophonists keep boxes of reeds for when a reed cracks or wears out, but there are no replacement parts for your vocal cords. If you want to have a long career, you must learn how to take care of your instrument.

In order for the vocal cords to vibrate freely, they need to be lubricated. Keeping yourself hydrated plays a major role in your body's ability to produce a thin layer of mucus that acts as lubrication for your vocal cords. You should drink at least 8 to 10 glasses of water every day. Aside from loading up on plenty of water, there are a host of things that you should try to avoid on a daily basis, but especially the day before and the day of a vocal performance.

✳ **Caffeine.** I know it's a bummer for serious coffeehouse folks, but caffeine depletes the body of water, making it harder to sing. The heart-wrenching list of caffeine-laced items includes many teas, coffee, chocolate, and most sodas.

✳ **Alcohol.** Along with its judgment-impairing aspects, alcohol also has a dehydrating effect.

✳ **Menthol Lozenges and Cough Drops.** Although the vapors from these items make your nasal passages feel good, they cause drying of your vocal cords.

✳ **Citrus Fruits.** Fruits such as oranges, lemons, grapefruits, limes, tangerines, pineapples, and tomatoes also cause dryness. It's time to dispel a big myth. Some people swear by drinking warm tea with a little honey and lemon. Please don't do it. Drinking the combination of these three things does have a soothing effect; however, they actually will cause drying. If your voice is feeling a bit worse for wear after the session, that would be the time to sip away, but by no means should you drink this concoction just before or during your session.

✳ **Antihistamines.** These are present in most over-the-counter cold and flu medicines. Though great when you are trying to clear congested nasal passages of the heavy mucus that usually accompanies a cold or flu, antihistamines not only clear the heavy mucus, but also eliminate the thinner mucus that your vocal cords require to function properly. Instead, try medicines like Nasonex or Flonase. They relieve the symptoms without the drying effect.

✳ **Smoking.** Tobacco and marijuana are serious irritants to the vocal cords. The heat generated from inhaling these items can burn the vocal cords. Can you say blowtorch?

✳ **Dairy Products.** Milk, cheese, yogurt, and other dairy products coat the throat, cause heavy mucus to build up, and cause post-nasal drip.

✻ **Ice-Cold Drinks.** Drinks that are too cold tense the vocal muscles. I recommend room temperature beverages (including water) just before or during a session. Hot tea is all right, too, if it is herbal, decaffeinated and, again, *without* the honey and lemon).

Another important factor in your vocal cords drying out is air conditioning. I make it a habit to ask for the air conditioning to be turned off while I am singing. Also, in places like Las Vegas, Nevada, where air conditioning is an everyday thing, I carry a portable humidifier. There are also vocal aids such as Throat Coat and Entertainer's Secret that are very effective at moisturizing the vocal cords.

Throat Coat is a tea that can be found at most health food stores. Go to www.traditionalmedicinals.com for more information.

Entertainer's Secret is a moisturizing throat spray. Go to www.entertainers-secret.com for more information.

Okay, to sum it up, to be a great lead vocalist requires some work and dedication on your part. Be prepared to spend countless hours honing your skills. Also, you will need to be disciplined in your lifestyle because the bottom line to good vocal health is eating healthy balanced meals, abstaining from or at least cutting back on certain items, and getting some exercise. Oh yeah, let's not forget the biggest ingredient to good vocal health—getting plenty of sleep. The body is an amazing self-healing mechanism when given enough rest, so make sure that you get the proper amount of sleep. Oftentimes your voice needs rest, too. The key is to know just when to *shut up!* As a matter of fact, I think I'll take a hint from that last statement and end this sermon right here.

Background Vocals

10

Singers such as Vesta Williams, Kelly Price, and Mariah Carey are among the many vocalists who began their careers as background singers. Most notably in pop, rock, and R&B music, background vocals are the audio glue that hold together the *hooks* for many hit songs. Background singers are heard more often than most people realize, yet they share a huge amount of anonymity.

ALL ABOUT THE SKILLS

Professional background singers also share skills that are often underrated, including skills such as:

* Being consistently on time for sessions
* Being mentally and physically prepared to sing upon arrival to a session
* The ability to stay alert for long periods of time
* Being able to take directions from the producer and/or section leader
* Quickly retaining vocal parts
* The ability to sight-read music
* Singing precisely in tune with other singers
* The ability to *blend* with other singers
* The ability to recognize one's own singing errors

Hook/Chorus: The part of a song that is repeated after each verse, typically by more than one singer and that gives it immediate appeal and makes it easy to remember. The term *hook* also has another, more metaphoric connotation—a phrase that was meant to catch the ear of the listener.

Blend: A balance of volume and timbre within a group of vocalists.

Being Early

I can't say it enough. To be early is to be on time, especially when there are other vocalists involved. Being on time is the best way to get your recording session started off right.

Being Prepared

If the client provides you with a CD, an mp3, a lyric sheet, a lead sheet, or a vocal chart, study the material carefully. I once did a session for which a couple of the singers did not study the parts, and, man, was it a nightmare. We all spent an extra hour with the producer trying to get these two singers on the same page. In the end, fortunately, the whole thing worked out, with the background vocals sounding incredible. Funny thing, though, I never saw those two singers on any of that producer's sessions again. Hmmm....

Upon arriving at the recording session, you have to be physically ready, too. Make sure that you get plenty of sleep the night before. Most background vocal sessions are marathons and not sprints. Believe me when I say that singing the same vocal parts over and over becomes a serious drain on your brain after a while. It is very easy to become bored. Plus, you will be standing in one place for long periods of time, so be ready by being fully rested.

We all have times when great things and bad things happen in our lives; however, producers generally can't afford to care. Don't get me wrong. I'm not saying that producers don't have genuine concerns about how you feel and what is happening in your life, because most do. But put yourself in their shoes. They are getting paid to do a job, which most often requires them to get things done in a timely manner and within a budget. Producers will often take a moment just to talk socially, but when it's time to work, keep in mind that it is important that you immediately get your head into the game.

Taking Directions

One of the hardest things to do is to take directions from someone you think is wrong, yet that's the dilemma that you will face sometimes in a recording session. Maybe the producer wants you to sing a part that has a minor 3rd in it against a major 7 chord. There have been a lot of sessions where I've found myself asking, "May I make a suggestion?" Sometimes the producer will say yes; other times you just have to bite your tongue and sing a part the way that you're instructed. The producer is always right, even if in truth that person may not know what the heck he is talking about. I always try to remember that the wonderful thing about getting paid to sing is that I'm getting paid to sing.

Quick Part Retention

On a high percentage of recording sessions in the pop music scene for background vocalists, the parts are learned by ear. The producers want you to be able to learn the song as fast as possible, get the parts recorded, and get you out of there as fast as possible. Short of that ear-training class that I keep talking about, I do have a couple of ways to practice what I call short-term memory.

The first method requires a singing partner with good singing skills and some imagination. Maybe you can get your voice coach to help you out. You will also need a metronome. I call this exercise "Call and Response." Put the metronome on a moderate tempo… say, around 70 bpm. Your partner then sings any made-up line.

Then, within a couple of beats, try to sing the line back. Your partner continues to make up lines and you continue to try to sing them back. As you get better at it, speed up the metronome.

The second method requires a bunch of used CDs. I still go to record stores that specialize in buying and selling used CDs, and I buy CDs from unknown artists of different styles. As I listen to the CDs, I try to learn all of the background vocal parts. Then I keep rewinding the song until I can sing all of the background vocal parts straight through without making any mistakes. The game for me is to see if I can learn each new song faster than the previous one.

Sight-Reading Music

The smaller percentage of the pop music scene will have charts (like those shown in Figure 10.1) or lead sheets waiting for you on the music stand. Don't get scared. Producers won't have you start to record cold, but they do expect you to be able to sing your parts as they appear on the chart during the rehearsal phase of the session. I have sung on a great deal of movie sound tracks, and for every session I have had to read music. Take a music theory class, or take my advice from Chapter 2 and purchase a music theory program for your computer. Most are very good and will teach you the basics of reading music.

Figure 10.1

Some producers will expect you to sing from charts.

Elements of the Blend

The hardest part for a group of singers performing background vocals is to sound like a cohesive group and not like individuals within a group. With that being said, there are a few producers who prefer that individualized sound. Most producers, however, prefer to go for a balance of different elements that comprise the blend:

Singing in Tune with Others

Sounds easy, but for many singers it is not easy to sing in tune with others. Your sense of pitch will be totally challenged in the studio, especially since there are any number of ways for background vocals to be recorded. There are, however, four common methods for recording background vocals, each with its own set of difficulties and solutions:

Everyone sings a different note in the harmony at the same time on one microphone. This is the most traditional way for background vocals to be recorded. Once one track is recorded, the producer usually *overdubs* a *double* track consisting of the exact same harmonies. Some producers may even overdub a triple track (or more) depending on the final sound they want to achieve. Listen to ws_10-01.mp3 on the companion Web site for a sample of how this recording method sounds.

Overdubbing: The process of recording new vocals, instrumental parts, or sound effects on additional tracks in synchronization with previously recorded tracks.

Doubling: Recording an additional track electronically or mechanically, duplicating the same material as recorded on the original track.

This presents a certain set of difficulties if one or more of the singers aren't used to singing harmony in a group. Hearing someone sing a harmony part different than what you are singing while standing next to that person can be distracting. It's easy to be pulled from your harmony part and wind up either singing the other person's part or singing out of tune. Unfortunately, there is no immediate solution in the studio other than replacing that singer.

However, there are two long-term solutions to try that I highly recommend if you are having this problem. One solution is to join your school, church, or community choir. You will get plenty of practice singing harmony parts while hearing other vocal parts around you. The helpful aid is that you will also have a group of people next to you singing what you are supposed to be singing. This will give you the opportunity to hear the relationships between the different harmony parts. The second solution is per my recommendation from Chapter 2: Try enrolling in an ear-training class.

Singing on the right note and in tune is only one element of the blend. The other elements really play a role in this method of recording background vocals. Because each singer stays on the same note throughout the overdubbing process, there is a tendency for individual voices to stick out. The less knowledge the group of singers has about blending, the more pronounced the problem. Some producers may try to fix the blend problem by having the singers switch harmony notes on subsequent tracks. This brings about a new singing responsibility and possible problem. When doing background vocals you need to know more than just your own notes in the harmony. A good background singer knows all of the harmony parts and is ready to sing any of the parts at a moment's notice. For some singers, this is very hard to do. Once these singers learn their initial part, they then find it difficult to make the switch to another harmony. I wish that I had a quick fix to this problem, but, again, my suggestion is to enroll in an ear-training class.

Everyone sings in unison on one microphone and then switches to a harmony note, also in unison. Many producers use this way of recording background vocals for one of two reasons. Either they are trying to create a choir sound or they are trying to create a blended sound in which no single person's timbre sticks out. Usually this method is done by first putting the vocalists on one vocal part, singing in unison. Then the producer records the part as many times as needed to accomplish the desired effect. The producer then proceeds to have singers learn and record the next part, also in unison. This procedure continues until all of the harmony parts have been recorded. Listen to ws_10-02.mp3 on the companion Web site for a sample of how this recording method sounds.

This method brings to light the difficulties involved around singing in unison. I have found that if the timbre of one or more other vocalists is closely matched to yours (which for a lot of producers is the goal), it becomes hard to hear what you are singing and hard to discern if you are singing in tune. This is definitely the time to employ one of the headphone techniques I discussed in Chapter 8. Wear one side of the headphones off of your ear. This will help you to hear yourself a bit better. And make sure that you have that open side pressed against the back of your head to avoid feedback or bleed.

Everyone sings a different note in the harmony at the same time on different microphones. This method (see ws_10-03.mp3 on the companion Web site) is usually reserved for singing groups that perform live together all the time. Although it's one of the least used methods of tracking vocals, engineers sometimes like recording this way because it gives them control over certain elements of the blend. The biggest problem with this method is with the vocalists bleeding into each other's microphones. If the studio is large enough, this can be partially controlled with the use of gobos.

Each individual sings a different note in the harmony at different times on one microphone. This method (see ws_10-04.mp3 on the Web site) has become one of the most popular methods of recording background vocals in the pop, hip-hop, and R&B music worlds.

One vocalist goes into the studio and records and does overdubs, singing the initial vocal part. The next singer then goes into the studio and records and does overdubs singing the next part. And so it goes, until all the parts are recorded. This method relies less on the vocalists' blending skills and more on the producer's ability to guide each singer. The producer also must have the ability to correctly choose the right singer for each vocal part. The process gives both the producer and engineer total control over the blend. The resulting tracks can later be altered or edited in a way that accomplishes the desired production goal. Then, there is an alternative version of this method that I would like to mention... .

The lead vocalist sings all of the background parts. This method is the same as above, except that the lead singer or just one background vocalist sings all of the parts.

Volume

The initial objective in the volume department is being careful not to sing so softly as to not be heard or so loudly that you stick out in the group. The engineer will spend some time getting everyone to sing at the right volume levels. The engineer or producer will have each singer switch positions and move backward or toward the mic in an effort to find the right volume balance among all of the singers. Once the right positions have been established, it then becomes incumbent upon each singer to remember that position. If you think it will be difficult for you to remember your spot, try employing the painter's tape tip from Chapter 9.

Your volume plays a part in your timbre, too. Some singers start to sound a bit aggressive or brash when singing louder. Some producers may want that effect, but if not, you have to be aware of this and soften the tone by lowering your volume. If the engineer needs you to be louder but wants your timbre to stay as it is, he may just have you move a bit closer to the microphone. Once the proper level has been established, it again becomes your task to consistently sing at that volume.

Positioning

Back to the microphone again. Some microphones have different ways of listening than others. It is important to know the listening pattern of the microphone that the engineer is using. The microphone's listening pattern dictates where the vocalists should stand in order to get the best possible sound. Without knowing the microphone's listening pattern, it would be very easy for someone to stand in an area where the microphone can't hear accurately. This is called being off-axis and usually occurs when standing to the sides of the microphone, which results in a loss of high frequencies known as off-axis coloration. This is a normal function of the microphone, since it is trying to reject inappropriate sounds. There are three common microphone patterns: cardioid, bi-directional (figure eight), and omni. Notice in Figure 10.2 how each microphone hears sound (as indicated by the light gray areas).

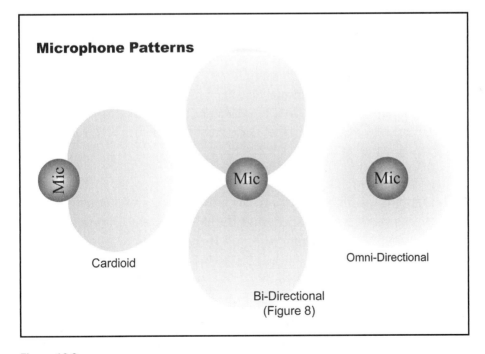

Figure 10.2

The basic listening patterns of microphones.

Word Pronunciation

Though the idiom of music or the producer's needs dictate how a lot of words are to be pronounced, the singers must pay close attention to each other to make sure that they are on the same page. Take, for instance, the words "with you." Depending on the style of music, those two words can be pronounced a number of ways: "with you," "wid you," "wid choo?", or "wit chyoo?" Take time to talk over the words with the producer and the other singers.

Timing

In the world of singing background vocals, there are two timing issues. The first situation deals with the same issue present with some lead vocalists: singing "off beat." For a quick review of the solution to this problem, take a moment now to refer to the section "Improving Timing" in Chapter 9.

 There are all kinds of metronomes that you can purchase. There is the old-school version with the pendulum that swings back and forth; there is the digital type that bleeps and makes an LED light up on the beat; and, for PDAs and computers, there are even software programs that make great metronomes.

The second timing issue has to do with the way you start and end phrases. Suppose, for instance, that the vocalists are singing a phrase with the lyrics, "hot summer nights." If the song is in *common time* and the word "nights" is supposed to be approximately four beats long, where does the sound of the "ts" happen? Does it fall on the last beat of that *bar*, just past the last beat of that bar, or on the one of the next bar? The result of this phrase not ending correctly would be multiples of the "ts" sound being pronounced at different times (see ws_10-05.mp3 on the companion Web site for an example).

Sometimes a singer within the group is assigned as the leader and will conduct the ending of certain words. Other times the producer will conduct the phrase endings. Just as with the word pronunciations, take time to talk over the phrase endings with the producer and the other singers.

Bar: Sections, typically of equal time value, into which a musical composition is divided.

Common Time: A rhythmic pattern in which there are four beats per bar, and the beat unit is a quarter note. This pattern occurs often in classical music and is the norm in rock, jazz, hip-hop, R&B, country, and bluegrass.

Vibrato

A background singer must have control over vibrato speed. There are even those instances where the need for a vocalist to sing without vibrato becomes paramount. If you have a group of vocalists all singing with different vibrato speeds, the result after a couple of overdubs adds to a disjointed sound. If that is the goal, fine, but most producers will want all of the singers to match their vibrato speeds as best that they can, or not use vibrato at all.

I have an exercise that is good for learning how to control the speed of your vibrato. It is a bit difficult to do at first, but with some practice it will become easier. You will once again need the guitar tuner that I recommended you use in the last chapter. While singing one long note into the tuner, start off singing with no vibrato. Next, go into a very slow vibrato. Then change the speed of the vibrato, getting faster piece by piece until you have the vibrato going as fast as you can. Then do the reverse until you get back to singing the note with no vibrato. As if that wasn't hard enough, here is the real hard part: do this in one breath with the extra goal of trying to keep it in tune. Check out the example ws_10-06.mp3 on the companion Web site.

> *"Background vocalists must have much more control over their voices than lead singers."*

Own Up to Your Singing Errors

In the studio, the phrase "It wasn't me" is a possible argument starter. That's a phrase that's best left to grade-school kids trying to stay out of trouble. There seems to be an unspoken code in the professional background vocalist community that you own up to your mistakes. Since you've no doubt been paying attention throughout this book, you should recognize the phrase "Sorry, my fault." You will get more respect from your fellow singers by owning up to your mistakes than by trying to duck the blame or, worse yet, pointing your finger. It also gives the producer an opportunity to possibly help you fix the problem.

ONE MORE TIP FOR HEADPHONES

Let's see, we've discussed the cue mix, the positioning of the headphones, volume, feedback, and bleed. What's left? Oh yeah, there are times when the producer may ask you to sit out on a part for any number of reasons. It could be that he just wants a smaller ensemble to sing a couple of parts. The thing to remember is that if you are going to step out of the studio, unplug your headphones, or, if you have the option, turn them all the way down. Doing so will prevent bleed or possible feedback.

THE FEELING

When singing background vocals, you don't have the option of bringing original style, feeling, and attitude to a recording session.

That is mostly within the domain of the lead vocalist. Background vocalists have to go by a combination of what the producer wants, what the lead vocalist has already tracked, and what the song calls for. If the song has a sad feeling to it, your job is to add to that emotion. If the lead vocalist is singing with a serious attitude, the producer may need you to copy that mood. It helps to read through the lyrics to a song to get an idea of what the story is about and, moreover, to understand the type of emotions that the song is supposed to convey.

As you have probably surmised by now, being a background vocalist is a technically challenging job—one that in many ways requires more skills than that of a lead vocalist. Did I say that? Oh, well…. It seems to me that background vocalists must have much more control over their voices, because the demands placed upon them to be perfect are infinitely greater.

Thoughts from a Few Professionals

11

I try to constantly stay in touch with many of my professional colleagues, mostly for no other reason than just friendship. Along with a lot of good-natured banter, we often talk about the many changes in the music business and how the changes affect our prospective careers. After a few of these thought-provoking conversations, I realized that it would be a great thing to include some of their comments and advice in this book. So, this chapter is comprised of interviews with some of my professional colleagues. Some of these music professionals have been in the business as long as me, or even longer, so please take advantage of their years of experience and wisdom. And don't discount the young pros. As you will see from the first interview, being young doesn't always equate to a lack of professional wisdom.

LEDISI—CREATING A LEGACY

Throughout my singing career, I have encountered many incredible recording artists. However, there is one who truly stands out among others: Verve recording artist Ledisi (pictured in Figure 11.1). Part of her appeal is that of a very gifted young vocalist with an old soul that is revealed whenever she engages the audience with her powerhouse alto voice. The appeal continues by way of the phenomenal musicianship she displays while performing.

Ledisi has worked with Moby, The Roots, Rockwilder, Boney James, Will Downing, Maysa Leak, Meshell N'degeocello, Chaka Khan, The Funk Brothers, and so many more. She also shares the distinct honor of being one of only two vocalists to appear as a guest artist on the Grammy nominated album, *Luther Vandross Tribute (Forever For Always For Luther)*. Now with two remarkable CDs under her belt, she is poised for a new musical adventure with her new label, Verve Records. Over a couple cups of caramel macchiato, Ledisi kindly shared with me some of the remarkable highlights of building her career.

Figure 11.1

Ledisi.

CLAYTOVEN: Please tell me about Ledisi.

LEDISI: Well, I'm a singer in the Bay Area. I've been an underground artist for probably about 8 years, and finally I'm signed to a major label. I've been doing theater, studio recording, and live performance. My live performances are mostly how I'm known.

Originally, I'm from New Orleans, Louisiana. My family moved here to Oakland, California, where I was raised. Oakland is where I pretty much learned most of my funknicity; that's what I'm gonna call it. [laughter]

I studied classical at YMP (the Young Musicians Program in Berkeley, California), while also studying at Skyline High School (at the time it was gonna become a performing arts school). So, I was learning a lot of different types of music, show music and other music. I kinda got the performance bug with that. While learning classical, I was also learning how to sing gospel, 'cause I didn't grow up on gospel. I grew up learning Chaka Khan and Rufus; Earth, Wind & Fire; Norman Connors; that kind of music. Then I learned jazz in college. I learned everything backwards.

CLAYTOVEN: You just briefly mentioned college. How much formal education did you have?

LEDISI: I never finished college because I started to work, but I was working as a singer. So, I was working nights and trying to spend the days at school. I went to Chabot College and California State University in Hayward. Although I never finished school, I would have loved to, but I guess it all worked out how it was supposed to.

CLAYTOVEN: That's right. Things happen for a reason. So, what sparked the bug of being a recording artist?

LEDISI: Well, honestly, watching my mom. Because back then she would record in our tract house. We had the living room, my bedroom, my mom's bedroom, and then the kitchen and bathroom all in one shot—shotgun house. My mom was in a band, back in the day, called Carnova that was a soul–hippie thing. The band would record to an 8-track in the living room, and my mom would record in my room. So, I watched my mom as she was recording. I would lie on the bed watching her sing. And I was like, wow! Seeing her on stage was one thing, but to see her actually record was a bigger thing. What did it for me was when I asked, "Mom, can you do that *cha-kow*" line for me while you're recording, please, please." I was begging her for that one little line to see if she could do it. Then she did. And when they played it back, my little line, I was so excited. I was like, "Mama, you did my line! And it's on the record." So, when they started pressing cassettes, I thought, wow, I could actually here it over and over and over again. To see that happen...oh, I wanted to do that.

CLAYTOVEN: From the point of view of a vocalist who's performing both live and in the studio, where do you see vocalists today?

LEDISI: I think from the performance element, singers don't have enough experience to develop their sound. Meaning performances in nightclubs, getting used to a crowd, getting used to when things sometimes mess up, getting used to improvisation, getting used to everything from the ground up. Unfortunately, many young singers don't have performing arts in schools to keep it going, where they can perform live and get used to people. Some are so nervous that they hide behind dancing or they hide behind imagery, and then the voice is lost. They look good, they sound good, but the voices aren't as strong as voices used to be. Remember, we had singers where you were captivated by the lyrics and the way they sang. You didn't care about the lighting show. Earth, Wind, and Fire, they put on a full-out show. Oh, and Phillip Bailey, if he didn't hit that high note on "Reasons," you'd be mad, right? The feeling you get when you hear those singers is what it was all about. Now, it's just about the dancing or what kind of outfit someone is gonna have on. The only person today that is perfecting it all is Beyoncé. She has the whole package, the look, the sound, and she can sing. If she stops dancing, she can still carry the same intensity. You know what I'm saying? I can't wait to hear her do some jazz or something classical. She is constantly reaching and still sounding like herself—with the elements of the old school, 'cause she's listening. You can tell when someone's listening and learning.

CLAYTOVEN: So, it sounds a bit like you're saying good studio singers come from really good performance singers, because they understand what it takes to perform. By the way, I think that you have the whole package as well.

LEDISI: Yeah, yeah, thanks. [laughter] I admire studio singers even more, because it's an art form. It is really hard. My first experience in the studio I tried to sing background vocals with two of the most fabulous background singers. I was whipped 'cause I could not get my part; I could not hold my part down. After that, I challenged myself and worked on it so I could be better. But that's a hard job, to consistently hit the same note, the same way, for a producer. That's what they're looking for, not adding each time, consistency. I learned from that. So, when it was time for me to record again, I was ready.

CLAYTOVEN: I've noticed that even though you say you haven't finished college, it seems to me that you have serious musician skills.

LEDISI: Over the past 4 years I've had to be on the road, working with six different bands, having to tell them what I need. Each band was totally different from the other. Even though I do play the piano and, luckily, have a background in music theory, I had to make myself sit down and learn how to communicate with musicians. You have to study. Even if you don't stay in school for music theory the whole entire time, you will have to go back to it. No matter what, the piano is everything. You can sit down at the piano and decide what your chord changes are in a song, or at least what key you're in. Find out from other musicians what your key is if you can't read music. Write it down next to the song title and keep a little log. Those that don't know music, you have to start developing a way to communicate with other musicians. If you use the excuse, "Oh, they don't know my song," you're gonna be stuck or you're never gonna get the job.

CLAYTOVEN: You bring such emotion to the songs you sing. How do you do that?

LEDISI: I take the words and have the producer read them. Then I ask him, "What does that mean?" What does he feel when he reads that? What experience has the producer had that I can hear when I listen to him? I can now hear the story, and I go *oooh, I know what he means.* Then I need to sing it like a story, because if you don't sing it like a story, then your listener won't feel it.

Many singers don't pay attention to the words. When you pay more attention to the melody and memorization of the words, you forget that the words mean something. That's why I enjoy singers like Sarah Vaughn. She was clever at it. Carmen McCrae, clever. And I love Abby Lincoln's "A Turtle's Dream." Oh my God! The way she takes you there, [singing] *hey lordy mama, what cha gonna do?*

What you gonna do? It's a conversation, a singing conversation that you can feel in your ears. If I can't feel it in my ears, or in my heart, forget it.

CLAYTOVEN: One of the hardest things to do is to find your voice, find what makes you, *you*. Especially when everyone wants to categorize you in some kind of way. Ledisi, when I listen to your CDs, you definitely can tell from song to song who it is. And that is great because that is what makes the difference between a singer that comes out today and is gone tomorrow, or somebody like Aretha Franklin or Mariah Carey who has a distinctive sound and winds up being someone that every other singer is trying to copy. What was it that helped you to find Ledisi?

LEDISI: Well, all singers mimic to learn something. I've mimicked everybody just to find out how to get that sound, and also to prove to others that I can sing that way. I mean, that's what all singers do when first starting out. I can do that Anita Baker line or I can do that Mariah Carey high note. That's how we learn.

Performing live also helped me find my own voice. Then the challenge was how to calm it down in the studio. To still come across with the same passion is a difficult thing. Other singers that I knew started in the studio and already knew how to sing a certain way, but for me, actually recording myself was hard. How do I capture the same essence of what I do live without doing too much? What made finding my voice in the studio such a hard thing is I was always over thinking. The majority of singing is mental. When you think you can't do it, you can't. When you think you can, you can. I always believe that 'cause I come up with stuff in the studio that I thought I couldn't do. So, finding my own voice was a lot of pulling from other vocalists' sounds, listening to the instrumentation going on with my band, the vibe of the crowd's reactions to my singing, and recording myself and hearing it back.

You know, hearing yourself back is also one of the hardest things to do. You have to listen though, in order to find your own voice.

You have to listen to what you are doing, figure out where it's coming from and why you do that, as well as how to change the sound.

I never totally sing the same way, because I'm constantly hearing new singers that enhance what I have going on. For instance, when I started listening to hip-hop. Also, for a time I was just listening to R&B, jazz and gospel, and I interpreted my classical training as well. And, after taking a little bit of everything I learned, I mixed it up to make it sound like me. Then I started listening to instrumentalists for a long time. People think, oh, you're scatting from Ella. No, not really. I was listening to Coltrane and Bird, which was difficult to listen to 'cause they play a lot of notes. Then I started grabbing Ella's sound to mix it in, but I still sound like me 'cause I also added the hip-hop element that I like. I keep adding layer upon layer upon layer of what I listen to. You are what you listen to. If you only listen to a certain singer, you're gonna be that certain singer. But, if you take everything you learn like tabla music, techno, house, Brazilian music, Cuban music, Latin music, or whatever music you come across, you can mix it all together. And that's gonna be who the audience hears. That's how it happened with me.

CLAYTOVEN: How do you maintain that when you're dealing with a label?

LEDISI: That has been the fun part. I call it fun, but some might say a challenge. It's like putting a puzzle together. I'm finally on another layer that I thought I'd never have to go to because independently I just did what I felt. It was raw, it was fun, and that's what people liked. Now I had to think about, am I gonna compete with what's out there or am I gonna continue to be who I am. I've decided to continue to be who I am, and add little elements of what's already out there.

CLAYTOVEN: That's a good thing because the most successful artists are those who are trendsetters, and it's good that you see that.

LEDISI: That's why I started my company, Innovators For Timeless Music. That's what I'm trying to create, something that's timeless. Anytime you go to my show, or you see me live, or hear my records, you go, "Wow, I remember something like that," or "That reminds me of…," but it's still Ledisi. You can play my records years from now and it's still the joint. You know what I mean? That's what I want to be. That's how I want to leave here, having a legacy that's Ledisi.

For more about Ledisi, visit her Web sites, www.ledisi.com and www.myspace.com/ledisi.

JAN SMITH—HELPING STARS SHINE BRIGHTER

In my search to find the perfect vocal coach to interview, I've run across many wonderfully talented coaches, but none like Jan Smith. What makes this incredible vocal coach so unique? Well, she is not only an accomplished vocalist and vocal coach, but she also possesses serious skills as a vocal producer. Many successful recording artists, such as Rob Thomas, Latoya Luckett, and Usher will not go into the studio without her expertise.

Figure 11.2

Jan Smith.

I was fortunate enough to catch up with Jan Smith, or "Mama J" as she is affectionately known by many of her clients, one day before her birthday. Even with the excitement of birthday festivities only a few hours away, she was gracious enough to allow me an interview. I hope that you truly enjoy this awe-inspiring conversation.

CLAYTOVEN: I'd first like to get a little background on you and your studio.

JAN: Jan Smith Studios in Atlanta is a vocal coaching and artist development facility. I have four full-time vocal coaches and two part-time vocal coaches who basically cater to the needs of contemporary musicians. We kind of see ourselves as personal trainers for today's vocal athletes, meaning we take people on who are performing, writing, and recording anything from R&B and hip-hop, to rap, country, pop, heavy metal, rock and roll, alternative music. Anything that's in the contemporary medium that is non-classical or opera is what we do. The way we do that is by doing a personal hands-on assessment to find out where the clients are from a functional, theoretical standpoint; what they know, what they don't know about "music proper." Then we try to figure out the best plan of action to help them raise the bar for their personal best within the confines of who they are and what we feel they can accomplish. We also have a guitar instructor who works with singer–songwriters on music theory for better writing. So, we adapt our services to the needs of the kinds of clients.

CLAYTOVEN: Do you spend a lot of time in the studio with these artists?

JAN: Yeah, I own a full ProTools HD facility, which is next door to the coaching facility. It makes my life easier to be able to walk out of the coaching side and into the recording studio to work with artists on vocal production and recording. We also do a lot of vocal pre-production on the coaching side to get people prepared to record the material, whether I'm the producer or not.

My personal schedule is reserved for more of our national and touring artists. So, I'm working with Usher, India Arie, or Rob Thomas, people like that, depending on what phase of their career they're in. If they're getting ready to go into the studio to record, then I'm doing vocal pre-production and helping ready them for going in to record. If they are preparing for a tour, that's a whole different mindset, an entirely different way of training, if you will.

CLAYTOVEN: What are some of the common needs of vocalists today trying to get into the studio?

JAN: The biggest issue for most vocalists is lack of information. It's not so much that people aren't functional with their singing, but they could be so much better and less encumbered with bad habits if they knew, if they really understood the function of the body and how it sings, and the vocal cords. I mean, most people don't even know how many vocal cords they have or where they're located or what they're made out of. And if you don't know those simple basics, how can you then manipulate your body to get it to do what you want it to do, whenever you want it to. So, information/education is a big thing. Just helping people to know what they're doing is a huge part of what we do. Past that point, it's about conditioning.

It's just like getting an Olympic athlete ready for a major competition. Most singers use their voices all day long to talk and yell and scream. Then they expect their voices to compete in an Olympic "singathon" by doing gigs five nights a week. The physical material may not hold up depending on how well they're taking care of themselves. So, conditioning is a big part of it.

Then you have pitch and interval issues that people really need to dig in deep on. Fine motor control issues, being able to *riff*, and being able to improv and hear harmonies are big items as well.

CLAYTOVEN: Do you find that a lot of the singers today are learning about audio programs such as ProTools and what can be done with these and other programs like AutoTune? Are they a little bit lazier than singers of the past?

JAN: Well you know, it's been real interesting. I think that there are some singers that obviously rely on technology too much. The problem with that is when they stand in front of people and have to deliver live, they can't do it. The wonderful thing about working with true artists, people like Usher and Rob Thomas, is they use their time in the studio to learn. We all know that vocals are corrected, because everybody has the technology, and that's what we do. But, when you go to see Usher perform, he's every bit as good live as he is on his recordings. That's a person who studies the art of technology. Rob will study his recorded vocals so that he's a better singer when he goes on tour. It makes him a better performer all the way around. If you've listened to people like that over a series of several years, then you understand that they are continuously studying, using technology to their advantage to make them better performers. The proof is in the pudding. If somebody walks on stage and they suck, then it's not hard to figure out, well okay, some producer just *comp'd* a good vocal track. Good for them, but that ain't the singer being good.

Riff: A short melodic phrase, usually improvised by an instrumentalist or vocalist.

Comp Track: Short for composite track. A final track that is made up of various parts or elements of other tracks.

CLAYTOVEN: I'd like to go back a little bit. How did you get interested in this part of the business?

JAN: Being an artist myself. I grew up being the kid who wrote a song when I was nine years old, cut my first record when I was fifteen, and was touring with bands by the time I was seventeen. It's my lifestyle. I've been in studios and performing and writing my entire life. Because I was known as a good vocalist throughout the southeast, a gentleman who owned a rock guitar school asked me to help one of his students who was struggling vocally. I thought that I could probably help figure out why the guy was losing his voice, and kinda did that, and got known for helping "street musicians." You see, at that time, which was about twenty years ago, nobody was catering to the needs of rock singers. There was nothing available for musicians who were singing in clubs and doing all kinds of contemporary gigs. I kind of got known as the "go-to girl" in the industry for that. Eventually, labels began calling me to help with their developing and touring artists, and the rest, as they say, is history. God is good, and I've been blessed beyond measure in this endeavor, but it really all started by me helping somebody else, and the door just flung wide open.

CLAYTOVEN: What other types of things did you do in your career as a singer?

JAN: I had a pretty good run as an artist in the southeast and the eastern seaboard. Played with several different bands and then eventually ended up heading the group that was under my name, The Jan Smith Band. We toured, and now I have six albums to my credit. Mostly, if you like Bonnie Raitt, then you would probably like me. My style is very reflective of my southern gospel upbringing and the blues rock music I grew up listening to. I still perform now, but mostly only when I want to. I still write and record, and obviously I'm involved in production working with other artists. There's still a large portion of my life creatively stimulated that way.

CLAYTOVEN: What type of training did you have coming in as a singer?

JAN: It started with growing up in the Southern Baptist churches. You know, gospel choirs and being influenced by the church, the four-part harmonies and all the great music therein. From there, the public school systems. I'm a classically trained flautist of sixteen years. I played in high school marching bands and symphonic bands. I also trained in the choral programs throughout junior high and high school, performing in All-State choruses, etcetera, and picking up some individual training as I went along. But my formal education is actually in psychology. I'm the only person on my staff that doesn't hold a degree in music.

CLAYTOVEN: I can relate. I was originally trained as an oboist and clarinetist. How important do you think that training as an instrumentalist plays into what you do as a vocalist?

JAN: I think it helps a lot. I don't think you need to learn calculus to balance your checkbook, but I do think that understanding how to basically add and subtract, multiply and divide helps you to get around. So, I think that if a vocalist knows a little bit of basic music theory, what I consider layman's theory, and learning the numbers system *(Number Chart System)*, it helps give them a reference. I think it's incredibly important that instructors try to educate vocalists in a way that is applicable to the vocalists' style of music and lifestyle. I think that probably the biggest disservice of a lot of instructors is that they don't meet people where they are. Here at Jan Smith Studios, that's kind of our moniker. It's our goal to really meet people where they are and then take them from where they are to where they want to be.

Number Chart System: A shorthand method of writing musical arrangements, originally developed by Nashville studio musicians. The method involves reducing a chord chart to equivalent numerical expressions.

CLAYTOVEN: What things do you recommend vocalists do, just in general, in trying to really hone their skills as a studio vocalist?

JAN: Well, the studio is a different animal than performing live. I think it's an entirely different environment. You really have to understand how to bring the performance to the microphone as well as understand the technology that's being used so you can use it to your advantage. I would tell most vocalists if they want to have great studio performances to understand good microphones and the microphones that sound best on their voice. Vocalists have to understand the different spectrums, parameters, and electronics of those mics, because not everybody's voice sounds good on the same microphone. There is also whether or not to compress a vocal and the different types of EQ that you can use. There are so many factors in the studio that can enhance the vocal, but can also make it sound like crap if you don't know what you're doing. I guess my biggest concern is that there are so many vocalists that don't understand those properties, and so they rely on the person sitting behind the board, the engineer or the producer, to know their voice best. I think that's wrong. I think vocalists should be educated. They should be the ones who sit down with the producer and say, "Hey, my voice sounds best on this kind of mic." I think it's the vocalist's responsibility to understand his body, his sound, and his instrument in the same way that guitar players know different gauges of strings, and drummers know sticks and drum heads. Vocalists, by and large, don't care and are kind of ignorant to the process.

CLAYTOVEN: Even going beyond that, for instance guitarists knowing their amps and the electronics involved with recording their instrument, don't you think it's just as important for vocalists to learn at least the basics of digital audio programs like ProTools?

JAN: Oh, absolutely. The fact that I'm considered to be an extraordinary vocalist makes me even more extraordinary as a vocal producer, because I know how a vocalist should sound, where a breath should take place, and how the phrasing should be. It makes me better at being able to put together flawless performances for other vocalists. I guess artists, myself included, kind of hate ProTools and AutoTune for that reason, but as a producer I love the technology. It allows me to show people what they're capable of. The best of the best of what they have to offer can then be put together in a way that makes the artist sound like they did it in one take. It makes them proud and it gives them something to learn from and strive for. Vocalists today have no excuse not to immerse themselves in all that is available to make them better and smarter than they are.

 To check out Jan Smith's impressive client list and for more information, visit her Web site, www.jansmith.com.

LESLIE ANN JONES—I REALLY LIKE SINGERS

In 1983, I was hired to sing background vocals on the song "Love For Love" for the Whispers. When I got to the session, which was at The Automatt Studios in San Francisco, the first person I met was Leslie Ann Jones (pictured in Figure 11.3). She was the first female engineer I had ever seen, and to this day remains one of the most talented engineers, male or female, that I've ever met. Even during those early days when we first met she had already built a reputation for being the queen of recording vocals. She has continued to prove why she wears that crown of distinction with flawless recordings of artists such as Rosemary Clooney, Bobby McFerrin, Bebe Winans, and Luther Vandross. Years later, Leslie Ann has become a true Renaissance woman in the field of engineering, having worked on numerous films, television programs, and commercials, as well as records.

Currently, Leslie Ann Jones is the Director of Music Recording and Scoring for George Lucas's Skywalker Sound complex in Northern California, where she still records and mixes for a variety of projects. She took a break from her intense schedule to chat with me briefly about her career and offer some revealing insight into recording vocalists.

Figure 11.3

Leslie Ann Jones.

CLAYTOVEN: How did you get started as an engineer?

LESLIE ANN: I was a guitar player and a singer in bands when I was a teenager, and when one of the bands I was in split up, I ended up with a PA system. Then I started doing live sound for bands, and formed a live-sound company with a couple of friends of mine after pooling our equipment. In like 1970 or '71 I had a studio in my home, and it was that point that decided I preferred doing sound rather than being a guitar player. So I started pursuing a career in recording.

CLAYTOVEN: Throughout all the years, you've been known as the killer vocal engineer. What is your secret?

LESLIE ANN: I think it's that I really like singers. I know that sounds kind of silly, but, my mother was a singer. Singers surrounded me when I was growing up, both going to see them perform live and also hearing them on records. My parents had a Lincoln Continental with one of the first 8-track tape players in it. My mother had cartridges with Tony Bennett, Barbra Streisand, and all those great singers. So I grew up with an early appreciation for singers. And then I was a background singer, although I wouldn't really consider myself in that league of singers by a long shot. So, when I started recording, I really had an appreciation for singers—

phrasing and all that. I think that enabled me to be seen as an engineer that was really good with vocals. I didn't set out to work hard at that. I probably worked harder at getting a great drum sound than I did at recording vocals. But, I guess just having had that experience helped me.

CLAYTOVEN: Who are some of your favorite vocalists to record?

LESLIE ANN: One session comes to mind with Bebe Winans. I worked on a session with him when I was an engineer at Capitol Records. He and Cece were in town to do some concerts and he wanted to do some vocals for a new album. So he came in and we went to work. He's a great singer. Also having a chance to work with Luther Vandross was fantastic. And, of course, there was all the time I spent with Rosemary Clooney.

CLAYTOVEN: What makes those singers such a standout?

LESLIE ANN: Well, I think preparation is probably the common thread that runs between all those people. They came in and knew exactly what they were supposed to do. In Rosemary's case, she would come in, sing one take to warm up, and maybe two more takes, and that was it. You had to get her vocal in three takes. Bebe has such a wide range, along with the emotions that he could put into the songs. It was the same thing with Luther. Oh, and I would also add somebody like Renee Fleming, who I had the chance to record just for one day. That was a real thrill for me because I'm a huge fan of hers. You know, she just opens her mouth and there's nothing she does that's not fantastic. But, I think the biggest thing is the fact that they were all prepared.

Singing in a studio is not easy. It's hard work. All of your flaws show up and it's really hard to sing naturally in a room with a microphone in front of you.

CLAYTOVEN: It seems to me that what makes you such a good vocal engineer is that you have a true love for vocals. I think that's a big thing, because it's hard to find a really good engineer to record vocals, someone who really understands vocals.

What steps do you go through to choose the right microphone for vocalists?

LESLIE ANN: Well, I'm pretty lucky because I have worked in studios with great microphone collections, both at Capitol Records and Skywalker Sound. Even when I worked at The Automat I had the luxury of putting up a couple of different mics. Hearing a vocalist on all of those mics enabled me to pick out the right one. Now that I've been doing this for so long I have an idea what a couple of different mics sound like.

The most important thing for me is to pick the right mic for a female vocalist, because it might not necessarily be the same mic choice as for a male vocalist. I think that a lot of engineers miss that. They just put up a mic that they think is gonna sound good on a vocal without thinking about the kind of vocal being recorded. Women tend to have more mid-range in their voice. And because there is less grit to their voice, when they sing louder it can be a little harsher than a man's voice. Guys have a lot more power, but might need some help with clarity. So, what gender the singer is and what type of music they're doing dictates what mic should be used. For instance, you could take a Neumann U-47 that might sound great on Rosemary Clooney, yet might not sound great on someone else, because it might have characteristics that aren't complimentary to that other person's voice.

CLAYTOVEN: What are some of your favorite microphones?

LESLIE ANN: The only mic that I found recently that sounds great no matter who I put it on we bought at Skywalker a couple of years ago, a Telefunken 251. I never really had much experience with 251s because none of the studios I worked in had one, and yet I knew many people that would always rent one. So, when one came up for sale, Skywalker was able to snag it. Further, I would say unconditionally that a Telefunken 251 and a Neumann M-149 are probably my two choices now that I would put up no matter who it was. Either of those mics might sound just fine. That's it right now, although I'm continually surprised.

I was in Hawaii doing a live recording with singers I had never worked with. We did the orchestra dates in the morning and then recorded some popular contemporary Hawaiian singers in the afternoon. It was people I had never really heard; also I had a limited choice of microphones. There was only one Tube mic, and that's the one that I ended up using. It was actually a Neumann M-147, which is not something I had ever used for vocals in the studio. I tend to use that microphone for other things, but it happened to be the only tube mic I had. Here at Skywalker Sound, I've been so lucky to have such a great mic collection.

CLAYTOVEN: What is the difference in recording vocals for film as opposed to television or for commercials or for records?

LESLIE ANN: Usually when you do vocals for film, you're doing vocals for end credits. So the overall mix itself is going to be different. For me, it probably has less to do with the sound of the vocal as it has to do with the overall mix. But, if you're recording a vocal that is actually going to be in a movie, then you're competing with dialog and sound effects and a lot of other things. So there are some considerations in terms of making sure that the balance of the vocal is right and doesn't compete with the other stuff. When recording vocals for commercials, I would probably not spend so much time on a real high-end sound. I might grab a really good sounding condenser mic, that can take a lot of level, to record a vocal sound really quickly. Something I know is going to pop out over the track. Because commercials are something that really need to kind of command your listening environment if the advertisement's going to sell product.

CLAYTOVEN: What advice do you have for aspiring vocalists trying to get in the studio?

LESLIE ANN: I would say two things. The first thing is to learn how to read music, which is extremely important. There is a big band record I'm going to do in a couple of weeks; they were planning on putting the singers on afterwards. But, they were hoping that I could do the tracks before they put the singers on. So, I had to tell them that I didn't think that was a very good idea, because not having a vocal to hear when I was mixing tracks was going to make it sound not as good if they put the vocal on later and then just kind of laid the vocal in. So, I suggested to them that they find somebody to do reference vocals, and the first criteria for something like that is somebody who can read, because there's a melody that you're supposed to sing. So, if you want to make a career out of singing in film scores and things like that, all that stuff is written out. Very few people have time for improvisation doing that kind of stuff.

And the second thing is to be as prepared as you can. If you're being asked to sing on a commercial, maybe try to get a rough mix of the demo before you come in so that you know what's expected of you.

To find out more about Leslie Ann Jones and Skywalker Sound, visit www.skywalkersound.com.

NARADA "MICHAEL" WALDEN—IT'S ABOUT THE MAGIC

It was in 1986 when I found myself singing for Narada Michael Walden (pictured in Figure 11.4) for the first time. An old friend of mine, Gigi, recommended me. Three days after a call from Narada's staff, there I was at Tarpan Studios singing on George Benson's *While The City Sleeps* album. As it turned out, that session was only the beginning of a long association with Narada. Over the years, I have had the honor of witnessing first-hand the magic that this multi-Grammy and Emmy Award-winning producer brings to the studio. Whether helping emerging talents find their voice or helping established stars refine their signature sound, Narada "Michael" Walden continues to guide musical artists toward commercial success.

Figure 11.4

Narada "Michael" Walden.

I had a unique opportunity to have a sit-down talk with Narada at Tarpan Studios, his recording facility in San Rafael, California. He gave me his enlightening thoughts on professional studio vocalists.

NARADA: First, let me say something about Claytoven. Claytoven, you are one of the finest musicians, period. You can sing in tune and can hear in tune. I mean, a lot of people can say they have relative pitch, but you not only have perfect pitch, but you know what to do with it, and what not to as far as arranging. You know what sounds good as far as harmonization to make a hit record. Many of the hits I've made in my career were done with your expertise and wisdom. You're one of the few guys I know that can be on the opposite side of the glass and can help me. I can say to you, "Listen, are you feeling this particular harmony?" or whatever I might hear and feel. I can always bounce my idea off you and you give me the right answer—what's gonna be the best sounding thing for the hit. Say, for example, when I get a demo and it's got tons of *stacked* harmonies, your ears are so finely tuned that you can hear every harmonization going down. Like that of *Take 6*, even with sophisticated, deep, thick harmony, you can hear all the parts. Now, that's a God-given gift. And you're famous for that; you're famous for being able to hear anything. I can just say, "Well, what is it? What are they doing in there?" You go, "Okay, let me show you what they're doing." You'll break down the actual parts for the other singers. That's a real skill.

 Stacking: (Also Overdubbing.) The process of recording new vocal or instrumental parts or sound effects on additional tracks in synchronization with a previously recorded track.

CLAYOTVEN: Thanks Narada. Now that I'm totally embarrassed [laughter], let me return the favor. You have a reputation of being one of the premier vocal producers. Part of that production prowess is in your ability to get the best out of a singer, even to the point where even the singer, when listening back says, "Wow, I didn't know I could do that." Now that is a skill! What is your take on what it is that you do?

NARADA: There are a few techniques I've developed over the years. One you know all about because you were in on a lot of these sessions. I move at a fast pace. Once the singer has opened up and is really singing, then the spirit kind of takes over. Now the spirit is only going to burn hot for a good hour, maybe an hour and a half, two hours max. Knowing that, I want to get the singer to do as much as I can while everyone is happy and in a jovial mood. I feel like if I can roll takes quicker than the singer's mind has time to analyze those takes, then I can get performances that maybe I wouldn't get otherwise. Whether it's Whitney Houston, Aretha Franklin, or whoever I work with, I've found that once they get excited or happy, I want to record as much as I can at that time, because at that point it's not about the mind.

Let's say it's the ending of a song where the singer is doing all the ad libs. I want to work backwards to forwards. I want to get the ad libs first, because if I first start working on a verse, the singer will get all analytical about how the lines should be. And the spirit will go away. Then when I need the fireworks for the ending, it's gone. So, I go in the studio purposely thinking "fireworks." Once they get excited, give me the fireworks. Go crazy, just give me all the juice. Then we can go back when the singer is kind of calm and get a little analytical about whether the second line of the third verse, or second line of the second verse, or first line of the first verse was the best it could be. That's the main technique I like to employ, because when singers have time to analyze, they will slow themselves down. That's really what it is, the singer's best stuff happening too fast to try to go back.

To new singers, I say pretend you're at the Grammys. Pretend Mariah's been on, and Aretha's been on, and now it's your turn. It changes things when they think, "Oh, my God, Mariah and Aretha have been on. I'd better sing some stuff." And then they do. So, I've gotta make new singers think that way, because in the studio we want to capture something magical. I'm aware of that magic.

And, speaking of magic, there are gears of magic. There's powerful chest-voice magic, and then there's head-voice magic. Singers use the head-voice magic a lot when it comes to things like what you've done for me, singing background vocals. This is where I want all the singers to be blended and angelic. That way if I make the background vocals really loud in the mix, I still get space for the lead singer. People don't realize that singing head voice is one of the hardest things to do. Singers have to sing over and over again, and in tune. That's why I always love working with you, because you're really one of the best at that. So, those gears are the things I'm really conscious of: chest voice, head voice, and then capturing that magic quick.

CLAYTOVEN: What do you feel makes a great lead singer, especially in the studio, because it's different from singing live?

NARADA: Although, having said that, some of the best live singers are usually the best studio singers. It's a rare exception when they're not. Mainly because people who do a lot of live singing have control over their voices, which I need for the studio. All those little riffs and licks and things, it's beautiful to have, to hear those nuances by someone who's really a professional. They're bringing their years of experience to the table. Like a Patti Austin, who can bring that live thing to the studio because she's a seasoned performer.

Aretha Franklin will warm up by singing the song through completely down the octave four or five times, over and over. Then she'll say, "Okay, now I'm ready." Now, when she says she's ready, that means that first take she's *blowing*. Aretha is a great live performer, and she brings all of that skill to the studio.

There's one other thing I want to say about Aretha. She comes to the studio prepared, having memorized what she wants to do. There is no lyric sheet on the music stand for Aretha, and I found that out the hard way. I went into the studio to make a correction of a lyric and there was no music there. There was nothing there, but just a blank stand. I was really impressed that she was so together to have memorized her work, which you rarely see anymore when you're talking about being prepared for the studio. Singers come in not knowing their music, not knowing anything necessarily. I'm not talking about background sessions where you're paid to come in and sing a part you're given. I'm talking about when it's your record, you should know your song. Many singers don't know their own songs. Now, Aretha, who is the queen, she really thinks about what she wants to say and what she wants to do. The great singers are prepared.

As great a singer as Whitney Houston is, at times she wasn't prepared. But, why did she sound so good? I played tricks with her. Songs were being thrown at her so fast that she didn't have enough time to study. So I had to walk her through the songs. I'd say, "Honey, just go to the mic and learn the first verse, and just sing the first verse a few times. Okay, now do the second verse two or three times. That's good. Here's the first chorus to learn. Now, do the first and second chorus. Okay, fine. And now in the out, just blow. Great, tomorrow when you come in let's do the song one more time because now you know the song." The next day Whitney would come in and blow. Later that day, the engineer and I would work all night long until 4:00 in the morning and comp the best bits of all her tracks. I would leave at 4:00 A.M., and then I'd have the engineer and studio crew stay until, say, 6:00 in the morning to spritz up everything and tune little things I wanted tuned. Finally a cassette would be dropped off to me. I would listen to it and let the boys go home and get 4 or 5 hours of sleep. They'd come back at noon and do any other little edits that I wanted done. Then when Whitney shows up, let's say at 3:00 or 4:00 in the afternoon, she's hearing a near-finished record. That's psychologically boosting for her, and she says, "Wow, it sounds done." Well, it almost is done. Eighty to ninety percent of it is done, because we spent all those hours to comp, to edit, and she's hearing the very best of her tracks. Now, she's so jazzed that she wants to sing a little something here or there, the finishing touches, and then we are done. Ninety percent of the songs I recorded with Whitney Houston were produced like that.

CLAYTOVEN: DAWs (digital audio workstations) are great tools for producers to get the best from every singer, but how is that affecting the singers of today?

NARADA: The editing process is a big deal in making records. It's not just what is sung, but it's also the comping—taking the best bits of what is sung. Today, with ProTools and AutoTune, that job has been made easy, because quite honestly, I always fix things. Maybe I shouldn't even say this, because it's sacrilegious to think of fixing Aretha Franklin. I mean, how do you fix Aretha Franklin? However, there are always at least little tweaks that I do. I want a song to sound good 20, 30, 50 years from now. So, if something sounds a little out to me, I'll fix it.

Yes, a lot of singers nowadays would never have a career if not for AutoTune and other tools like that. You have all kinds of kids making records, and producers and engineers are guilty for helping to make these singers sound fabulous. Then when you have great singers, they have to fight through all of the competition to even get heard, which is sad. So, yeah, this has definitely been a problem.

CLAYTOVEN: What do you look for in a good background singer?

NARADA: Ooh, I look to Claytoven. You are the best. You know how to blend and how to make the people around you blend. You're the ears and the chops, making sure everyone's on point and focused. If you're conducting, the other singers watch you for cut-offs, the breaths, the intonation, and all the other little things you're aware of that most singers don't even think about. The whole world is looking for you to conduct the sessions, to make the sessions flow. And if a harmony isn't working, you think of options. Have we thought of no harmony or just doing octaves? Those brain molecules percolating at a high velocity is what you bring to sessions. That's what I want from a background vocalist, someone that can bring something that's beyond all of us.

I also realized that stacking one's own voice is another art form. For example, look at Prince or Stevie Wonder. Look at Marvin Gaye and how great he was at stacking his own voice. He did all the harmonies. There was also a girl that I heard for the very first time when I was sixteen years old named Laura Nyro. She wrote "Stone Soul Picnic" and a lot of other hits. But, she was the first one I ever heard stack her own voice. I mean all the harmonies, and that was in '67. I was like, whoa!

I did a few sessions like that with Whitney Houston. You know, she didn't always have the patience to do it, but when she would, it sounded beautiful. Listen to the song, "For The Love Of You." All of those voices are Whitney. Beautiful. It's like heaven. Also, Mariah Carey insisted upon the background vocals being her voice on her records. I'd add more voices later if I wanted, but it had to be the blanket of her voice. And she was good at doing that. Prince is another singer I admire because he is really good at it too. And there's Michael Jackson with Quincy Jones. Quincy would stack 48 tracks that would be all Michael's voice. The combination of Michael being a great singer and Quincy being a genius when it comes to producing was awesome. And I have to be fair, the Beatles and the Four Tops, how they could stack their voices was an art form.

CLAYTOVEN: What do you foresee for singers in the future?

NARADA: Unfortunately, I see us still going more in the way where producers are making it easier for singers. It seems to be the thing that time is money and money is time. Singers want to come in, get it done, get out, and go do their live shows. They want to sing something through once or twice and go on with all their other various activities. So, producers are forced to have all of the tools and gimmicks behind the curtain, like The Wizard of Oz, to be able to fix things. If a singer doesn't come to me and goes to another producer, he'll have his bag of tricks. A lot of singers go to these producers so they don't have to work as hard. That's okay, because the audience knows that producers fabricate a bit, but the real test is when that singer walks out on to stage. What can they do live?

CLAYTOVEN: Do you think there's going to be more pressure for singers to have to come with it?

NARADA: Absolutely. Even back in my touring days, you had to come with it. In fact, you had to do your very best to blow all of the other acts off the stage. My band used to open for Chaka Khan and Rufus. We also used to open for the Brothers Johnson, and every night we'd try to smash them. That's part of the unspoken competition between artists. You have to have that killer instinct, because without it you will not survive in this industry. When Carlos Santana is on stage, he plays his guitar so hard you'll never forget him. Or, when Prince performs. He ain't gonna hit the stage unless something's gonna happen. Singers really have to cut the mustard, especially when the audience is paying top dollar.

CLAYTOVEN: What are the things singers need to improve?

NARADA: I would say intonation is key. I love vocals to be in tune. I am critical that way. But, having said that, I can always try to fix things. On the other hand, what I can't fix is soul and the feeling, which I rate as number one. Does a singer feel what they're singing? Does a singer have any understanding of what's coming out of their mouth? If a singer has empathy, or feeling for what's coming out of their mouth, I can damn near take anything and make it hopefully sound like something, if I feel it. Even a mistake can be genuine if it's felt. Aretha told me that.

I recall one time being in the session with Aretha. We were working on a verse, and the third line sounded a bit flat to me. She said, "Wait a minute." So she came into the control room and said, "Well, play it to me." So I played it and she finalized things by saying, "That's just the way I hear that." And you know, she was right. I mean, after I studied it, I realized that every inflection was great because of the feeling. I fell in love with it. Even more, it's on the hit song "Who's Zoomin' Who." So the most important thing to me is the feeling. Does it feel like your heart's broken? Are you crying some tears? Then cry those tears in the microphone, because if the song is supposed to make you cry, and if when you sing you don't, why should I?

 For more information on Narada "Michael" Walden, visit www.naradamichaelwalden.com.

Epilogue

Allow me to tell you one more story. Back in the days of going to school, playing in bands, and singing in choirs, I met a teacher who proved to be one of the most inspirational men I have ever met. My mentor, Bill Bell, was a teacher at Alameda Community College. Of the many music classes he taught at the college, my favorite was the stage band, of which he was the director. I loved playing the saxophone in that band. Because Mr. Bell was also a professional musician, there was the extra-added coolness of him being able to set up numerous public performances for the band. For some performances, he would break down the band into a small combo. He would occasionally talk me into singing leads that he had me learn. Reluctantly, I would sing, but as time went on I became more and more comfortable with it. He would pull me aside and talk to me about what he felt I was doing great and where I needed improvement. Then he would stick me out there again. I didn't realize it at the time, but he was giving me the push that I needed to not be afraid to take a chance with my talents.

I also remember that at the beginning of each school quarter, Mr. Bell had a speech that always concluded with, "Some people were meant to be carpenters. Some were meant to be plumbers. Some were even meant to be scientists. Well, starting today we will find out if you were meant to be a musician, or something else." That statement made the entire class cringe, but I knew why he said it. That was his way of making everyone decide, "Do I really want to do this?" It was his way of making everyone who truly wanted to be a musician focus. Now then, how about you? Do you feel that being a professional studio vocalist is what you truly want? I only ask because for you to be successful at anything in life you have to really want it and be willing to work hard.

I don't pretend to know it all; the music business is steadily changing, and as a result there is forever a learning curve. I do know that the first priority of all singers should be to continually educate themselves to the ins and outs of the music business. The more education singers have, the less likely they are to sell themselves short. Well, at this point you have taken a step toward that goal. By reading this book, you have at least proven that you have a serious interest in becoming a professional—that this may be what you really want to do. I hope that my small push—the knowledge you've gained from this book—will help you realize your dreams, and I hope that I've given you the courage to not let fear rule you, to look "No" straight in the eyes and not be discouraged, and to take chances with your talents. The rest of the work is up to you. Good luck, and I hope one day to sing with you on a future recording session.

Appendix

TRADE ORGANIZATIONS

AMERICAN ASSOCIATION OF ADVERTISING AGENCIES (4A'S)
405 Lexington Ave., 18th Floor
New York, NY 10174-1801
Phone: (212) 682-2500
Fax: (212) 682-8391
http://www.aaaa.org

A trade association of approximately 650 member advertising agencies, AAAA offers information and advice on all aspects of commercial production. Facilities include an extensive research library.

AMERICAN MUSIC CONFERENCE (AMC)
5760 Armada Drive
Carlsbad, CA 92008-4391
Phone: (760) 431-9124
Fax: (760) 438-7327
http://www.amc-music.com

This service organization distributes music industry information to amateur musicians and encourages their participation in various musical activities. Its supporters include record companies, ASCAP, and radio and television networks.

AMERICAN SOCIETY OF MUSIC ARRANGERS AND COMPOSERS (ASMAC)

P.O. Box 17840
Encino, CA 91416
Phone: (818) 994-4661
Fax: (818) 994-6181
http://www.asmac.org/

ASMAC represents the artistic and professional interests of arrangers, composers, and orchestrators; presents workshops and clinics for members and students; produces the *Take One* newsletter six times a year; and presents several annual awards.

ASSOCIATION OF INDEPENDENT COMMERCIAL PRODUCERS (AICP)

3 West 18th Street, 5th Floor
New York, NY 10011
Phone: (212) 929-3000
Fax: (212) 929-3359
http://www.aicp.com

AICP focuses on the needs, interests, and representation of commercial production companies in the United States. Founded in 1972, the organization represents 80 to 85 percent of all domestic commercials.

ASSOCIATION OF INDEPENDENT MUSIC PUBLISHERS (AIMP)

5 West 37th Street, 6th Floor
New York, NY 10018
Phone: (212) 391-2532
P.O. Box 69473
Los Angeles, CA 90069
Phone: (818) 771-7301
http://www.aimp.org/index.asp

A membership organization of independent record companies and wholesalers that provides resources, meetings, information, and legal assistance and acts as a go-between for major retail record chains and the music unions. AIMP also sponsors the Indie Awards.

CALIFORNIA COPYRIGHT CONFERENCE (CCC)

P.O. Box 57962
Sherman Oaks, CA 91413
Phone: (818) 379-3312
http://www.theccc.org

The CCC is a Los Angeles-based music industry organization whose membership is comprised of music publishers, songwriters, record companies, TV and film studios, attorneys, and accountants dealing with the music business. The CCC meets eight times a year, presenting speakers to discuss matters of interest to the music community on business, creative, and legal matters.

If you wish to be added to the CCC mailing list to be notified of upcoming events, or to join the CCC, please send your name and address to the address listed above.

CANADIAN COPYRIGHT OFFICE

Bureau of Intellectual Property
Consumer and Corporate Affairs Department
Ottawa-Hall, Canada K1A OE1
http://strategis.ic.gc.ca/sc_mrksv/cipo/welcome/welcom-e.html

You may request Canadian copyright applications and informational brochures through this office. The fee for each submission for copyright is $65 (Canadian) at present.

CHURCH MUSIC PUBLISHERS' ASSOCIATION (CMPA)

P.O. Box 158992
Nashville, TN 37215
Phone: (615) 791-0273
Fax: (615) 790-8847
http://www.cmpamusic.org/html/main.isx

CMPA publishes the free booklet *The Church Musician and Copyright Law* and provides other services. Call for more information.

COUNTRY MUSIC ASSOCIATION (CMA)

1 Music Circle South
Nashville, TN 37203
Phone: (615) 244-2840
Fax: (615) 726-0314
http://www.countrymusic.org

An international organization dedicated to the preservation, development, and promotion of country music. The CMA sponsors educational activities and presents awards in 20 categories in a televised ceremony.

FILM MUSIC NETWORK

Los Angeles Chapter
5777 W. Century Boulevard, Suite 1550
Los Angeles, CA 90045
http://www.filmmusic.net

The Film Music Network's Los Angeles and New York chapters host monthly networking events for the express purpose of helping professionals learn more about the industry, make contacts, and expand their businesses. Each month their events include guest speakers who discuss industry issues and subjects. Questions and participation from attendees are welcome. L.A. events are held the first Monday of each month; New York events are the second Monday. Call for location and membership information.

GOSPEL MUSIC ASSOCIATION (GMA)

1205 Division Street
Nashville, TN 37203
Phone: (615) 242-0303
Fax: (615) 254-9755
http://www.gospelmusic.org

An international service organization whose purpose is to preserve and promote gospel music. Members vote annually to present the Dove Awards in 20 categories.

HARRY FOX AGENCY, INC. / NATIONAL MUSIC PUBLISHERS' ASSOCIATION

711 Third Avenue
New York, NY 10017
Phone: (212) 370-5330
Fax: (212) 953-2384
http://www.harryfox.com/index.jsp

The Harry Fox Agency handles mechanical and synchronization licensing for copyrighted musical compositions and the distribution of royalties based on those licenses. Harry Fox Agency is a subsidiary of the National Music Publishers' Association, which addresses legislative and other issues about copyright, and regularly schedules meetings on topics of interest to the music community.

INDEPENDENT FEATURE PROJECT (IFP)

104 West 29th Street, 12th Floor
New York, NY 10001-5310
Phone: (212) 465-8200
Fax: (212) 465-8525
http://www.ifp.org

IFP is a non-profit membership organization that provides information services including panels; seminars; and conferences, including "Independents Night" (a monthly showcase of features, shorts, documentaries, and works-in-progress held in New York) and the Independent Feature Film Market (a festival held annually in the fall). The organization also has offices in Chicago, Minnesota, and Seattle. IFP's excellent Web site provides a wealth of information and contacts.

MOTION PICTURE ASSOCIATION OF AMERICA (MPAA)
15503 Ventura Blvd.
Encino, CA 91436
Phone: (818) 995-6600
Fax: (818) 382-1795
http://www.mpaa.org

The MPAA is a trade organization for the motion picture industry and is responsible for film ratings and other issues of industry policy.

NASHVILLE SONGWRITERS ASSOCIATION INTERNATIONAL (NSAI)
1710 Roy Acuff Place
Nashville, TN 37203
Phone: (615) 256-3354
Fax: (615) 256-0034
http://www.nashvillesongwriters.com/

This "world-wide resource for songwriters" is a non-profit trade association devoted to serving and protecting songwriters in all fields of music. It offers a network of 75 workshops in 34 states and four foreign countries.

NATIONAL ACADEMY OF RECORDING ARTS & SCIENCES (NARAS)
3402 Pico Blvd
Santa Monica, CA 90405

Phone: (310) 392-3777
Fax: (310) 392-2778
http://www.grammy.com

NARAS, also known as The Recording Academy, is dedicated to improving the quality of life and cultural condition for music and its makers. The Recording Academy is internationally known for the Grammy Awards and is responsible for scholarships, research grants, workshops, publications, and a career handbook.

NATIONAL ACADEMY OF TELEVISION ARTS AND SCIENCES (NATAS)

11 West 57th Street, Suite 600
New York, NY 10019
Phone: (212) 586-8424
Fax: (212) 246-8129
http://www.emmyonline.org

NATAS presents the Emmy Awards and other programs and seminars for the television industry.

NATIONAL ASSOCIATION OF RECORDING INDUSTRY PROFESSIONALS (NARIP)

P.O. Box 2446
Toluca Lake, CA 91610-2446
Phone: (818) 769-7007
http://www.NARIP.com/

NARIP promotes education, career advancement, and good will among record executives. It offers professional development opportunities, educational programs and seminars, the opportunity to meet and interact with peers, a job bank, a member résumé database for employers, a mentor network, a newsletter, and other services.

NATIONAL ASSOCIATION OF RECORDING MERCHANDISERS (NARM)

9 Eves Drive, 120
Marlton, NJ 08053
Phone: (856) 596-2221
Fax: (856) 596-3268
http://www.narm.com

NARM includes retailers; distributors; rack jobbers; major, major–minor, and independent labels; and cassette duplication companies whose primary income is from sales. It also sponsors promotional campaigns, lobbying, and the annual Gift of Music Awards.

NATIONAL MUSIC PUBLISHERS ASSOCIATION

711 Third Avenue
New York, NY 10017
Phone: (212) 834-0100
Fax: (646) 487-6779
http://www.nmpa.org

The National Music Publishers Association addresses legislative and other issues about copyright and regularly schedules meetings on topics of interest to the music community.

RECORDING INDUSTRY ASSOCIATION OF AMERICA (RIAA)

1330 Connecticut Avenue NW, Suite 300
Washington, DC 20036
Phone: (202) 775-0101
Fax: (202) 775-7253
http://www.riaa.com

The RIAA is a trade group whose member companies create, manufacture, or distribute more than 90 percent of all legitimate sound recordings sold and produced in the United States.

The mission of the RIAA is to protect and defend artistic freedom, promote strong intellectual property protection, combat record piracy, expand market access opportunities worldwide, meet the challenges of technology, facilitate the development of voluntary industry standards, and foster awareness of industry issues and products. The RIAA also administers the Gold, Platinum, and Multi-Platinum Awards Program.

THE SONGWRITERS GUILD (SGA)

1560 Broadway, Suite #1306
New York, NY 10036
Phone: (201) 867-7603
Fax: (201) 867-7535

6430 Sunset Blvd.
Hollywood, CA 90028
Phone: (213) 462-1108
Fax: (213) 462-5430

1222 16th Avenue South, Suite #25
Nashville, TN 37212
Phone: (615) 329-1782
Fax: (615) 329-2623
http://www.songwriters.org/new/home.htm

The SGA is an association of songwriters that helps to educate members and represents them with publishers and record companies. The SGA provides copyright information, administration services, and sample contracts.

UNITED STATES COPYRIGHT OFFICE

Library of Congress
Washington, DC 20559
(202) 707-3000 for information
(202) 707-9100 hotline for ordering forms
http://www.copyright.gov/

Copyright forms are downloadable from the U.S. Copyright Web site at http://www.copyright.gov/forms/. Write to request blank copyright registration forms of all types or booklets explaining copyright topics.

TRADE SHOWS AND CONVENTIONS

The International Music Products Association (NAMM), formerly National Association of Music Manufacturers
5790 Armada Drive
Carlsbad, CA 92008
Phone: (760) 438-8001
www.namm.com

NAMM is an international association that represents many retailers and manufacturers of musical instruments and products from all over the globe. It holds two conventions annually that feature showcases of new music products, seminars, and networking.

National Association of Recording Merchandisers (NARM)
9 Eves Drive, Suite 120
Marlton, NJ 08053
Phone: (856) 596-2221
Fax: (856) 596-3268
www.narm.com

NARM is a non-profit trade association that serves the music retailing community in the areas of networking, advocacy, information, education, and promotion. Its annual convention, called Insights & Sounds, features showcases of new product lines, seminars, and networking.

Audio Engineering Society (AES)
60 East 42nd Street, Room 2520
New York, NY 10165-2520

Phone: (212) 661-8528
Fax: (212) 682-0477
www.aes.org

A professional society devoted to its members who are exclusively in the audio technology field. It promotes research and commercial interests of designers, manufacturers, buyers, and users of professional and semiprofessional audio equipment. Its two annual trade shows (held in the U.S. and Europe) display most current makes and models of audio equipment.

Midem

11 rue du Colonel Pierre Avia
BP 572, 75726 Paris Cedex 15
France
Phone: 33 (0) 1 41 90 44 60
Fax: 33 (0) 1 41 90 44 50
E-mail: info.midem@reedmidem.com
www.midem.com

Midem is the world's largest music industry trade fair, held annually in Cannes, France. It features industry meetings, conferences, and seminars and provides an opportunity to meet with industry professionals in recording, publishing, live music, television, film, games, and more.

LABOR UNIONS

AMERICAN FEDERATION OF MUSICIANS (AFM)

Paramount Building, Suite 600
1501 Broadway
New York, NY 10036
Phone: (212) 869-1330
Fax: (212) 764-6134
http://www.afm.org

The AFM is a trade union that represents professional U.S. and Canadian musicians in collective bargaining and contract negotiations in all aspects of the entertainment industry.

AMERICAN FEDERATION OF TELEVISION AND RADIO ARTISTS (AFTRA)

New York National Office
260 Madison Avenue
New York, NY 10016-2401
Phone: (212) 532-0800
Fax: (212) 532-2242

Los Angeles National Office
5757 Wilshire Boulevard, 9th Floor
Los Angeles, CA 90036-3689
Phone: (323) 634-8100
Fax: (323) 634-8194
E-mail: losangeles@aftra.com
http://www.aftra.org/aftra/aftra.htm

AFTRA is a trade union that represents performing artists in radio and television in collective bargaining and contract negotiations.

ALBANY
(see Schenectady)

ATLANTA
455 East Paces Ferry Road, NE,
Suite 334
Atlanta, GA 30305
(404) 239-0131
(404) 239-0137 fax
atlanta@aftra.com

BOSTON
535 Boylston Street
Boston, MA 02116
(617) 262-8001
(617) 262-3006 fax
boston@aftra.com

BUFFALO
c/o WIVB-TV
2077 Elmwood Avenue
Buffalo, NY 14207
(716) 879-4989

CHICAGO
One East Erie, Suite 650
Chicago, IL 60611
(312) 573-8081
(312) 573-0318 fax
chicago@aftra.com

CLEVELAND
1468 West 9th Street, Suite 720
Cleveland, OH 44113
(216) 781-2255
(216) 781-2257 fax
cleveland@aftra.com

DALLAS/FT.WORTH
6060 N. Central Expressway,
Suite 468
Dallas, TX 75206
(214) 363-8300
(214) 363-5386 fax
dallas@aftra.com

DENVER
1400 16th Street, Suite #400
Denver, CO 80222
(720) 932-8228
(720) 932-8194 fax
denver@aftra.com

DETROIT
23800 West Ten Mile Road,
Suite 228
Southfield, MI 48034
(248) 228-3171
(248) 223-9223 fax
detroit@aftra.com

HAWAII
c/o AFTRA
260 Madison Avenue
New York, NY 10016
(866) 634-8100 (toll-free)
hawaii@aftra.com

HOUSTON
2000 North Loop W, Ste. 160
Houston, TX 77018
(713) 686-4614
(713) 688-4369 fax
houston@aftra.com

KANSAS CITY
P.O. Box 32167
4000 Baltimore, 2nd Floor
Kansas City, MO 64111
(816) 753-4557
(816) 753-1234 fax
kansascity@aftra.com

MIAMI
2750 N. 29th Ave., Ste. 200N
Hollywood, FL 33020
(954) 920-2476
(954) 920-2560 fax
miami@aftra.com

NASHVILLE
P.O. Box 121087
1108 17th Avenue South
Nashville, TN 37212
(615) 327-2944
(615) 329-2803 fax
nashville@aftra.com

NEW ORLEANS
c/o Miami Local
2750 North 29th Avenue, Suite 200N
Hollywood, FL 33020
(954) 920-2476
(954) 920-2560 fax
(866) 236-2941 (toll-free LA only)
neworleans@aftra.com

OMAHA
3000 Farnham St., Suite 3
Omaha, NE 68131
(402) 346-8384

PEORIA
c/o AFTRA
260 Madison Avenue
New York, NY 10016
(800) 638-6796 (National Broadcast
Dept. toll-free number)

PHILADELPHIA
230 South Broad Street, Suite 500
Philadelphia, PA 19102-1229
(215) 732-0507
(215) 732-0086 fax
philadelphia@aftra.com

PHOENIX
245 W. Roosevelt Street, Suite B
Phoenix, AZ 85003
(602) 265-2713
(602) 252-4713 fax
phoenix@aftra.com

PITTSBURGH
625 Stanwix Street, Suite 2007
Pittsburgh, PA 15222
(412) 281-6767
(412) 281-2444
pittsburgh@aftra.com

PORTLAND
1125 S.E. Madison, Suite 204
Portland, OR 97214
(503) 279-9600
(503) 279-9603 fax
portland@aftra.com

ROCHESTER
c/o AFTRA National
260 Madison Avenue
New York, NY 10016
(585) 467-7982

SACRAMENTO/STOCKTON
350 Sansome Street, Suite 900
San Francisco, CA 94104
(415) 391-7510
(415) 391-1108 fax

SAN DIEGO
c/o Los Angeles Local
5757 Wilshire Boulevard, 9th Floor
Los Angeles, CA 90036
(866) 634-8100 toll-free
(323) 634-8100 direct
(323) 634-8246 fax
sd@aftra.com

SAN FRANCISCO
350 Sansome Street, Suite 900
San Francisco, CA 94104
(415) 391-7510
(415) 391-1108 fax
sf@aftra.com

SCHENECTADY/ALBANY
c/o WGY-AM/WRVE-FM
1 Washington Square
Albany, NY 11205
(518) 452-4800

Shop Coordinators c/o WRGB-TV
1400 Balltown Road
Schenectady, NY 12309
(518) 346-6666
(518) 346-6249 fax

SEATTLE
4000 Aurora Ave., No. 102
Seattle, WA 98103-7853
(206) 282-2506
(206) 282-7073 fax
seattle@aftra.com

ST. LOUIS
1310 Papin, Suite 103
St. Louis, MO 63103
(314) 231-8410
(314) 231-8412 fax
stlouis@aftra.com

TRI-STATE
Cincinnati, Columbus, and Dayton, OH;
Indianapolis, IN; and Louisville, KY
920-A Race St., Second Floor
Cincinnati, OH 45202
(513) 579-8668
(513) 579-1617 fax
tristate@aftra.com

TWIN CITIES
708 North First Street
Suite 333 - Itasca Bldg.
Minneapolis, MN 55401
(612) 371-9120
(612) 371-9119 fax
twincities@aftra.com

WASHINGTON/BALTIMORE
4340 East West Highway, Suite 204
Bethesda, MD 20814
(301) 657-2560
(301) 656-3615 fax
wash_balt@aftra.com

SCREEN ACTORS GUILD (SAG)

New York National Office
360 Madison Avenue, 12th Floor
New York, NY 10017
Phone: (212) 944-1030

Los Angeles National Office
5757 Wilshire Blvd.
Los Angeles, CA 90036-3600
Phone: (323) 954-1600
http://www.sag.com

SAG is a trade union that represents performers in film, television, industrials, commercials, and music videos. This union helps actors with working conditions, compensation, and benefits.

SAMPLE DISCOGRAPHY

Claytoven's selected discography.

Claytoven Discography

This is a selected listing of the albums and sound tracks that I have performed on as a background vocalist.

Rent (Motion Picture Soundtrack)
Movie Cast
Warner Bros. • 49455

Ricky Martin
"Ricky Martin" (album)
C2Records/Columbia • CK 69891 • CD1

Jennifer Lopez
"On The 6" (album)
Work • WK 69351

Marc Anthony
"Marc Anthony" (album)
Columbia • CK 69726

Patti Austin
"In & Out Of Love" (album)
Concord Vista • CCD-4776-2

Kenny Loggins
"The Unimaginable Life" (album)
Columbia • CK 67865

The Temptations
"Phoenix Rising" (album)
Motown • 314530937-2

Celine Dion
"Let's Talk About Love" (album)
Epic • bk 68861

The Hunchback Of Notre Dame (Soundtrack)
All-4-One
Walt Disney • 60893-7

Barbra Streisand
"Higher Ground" (album)
Columbia • ck 66181

Mariah Carey
"Butterfly" (album)
Columbia • ck 67835

Hercules (Soundtrack)
Michael Bolton
"Go The Distance"
Walt Disney • 60864-7

Grover Washington
"Soulful Strut" (album)
Columbia • ck 57505

Jason's Lyric Soundtrack
Oleta Adams
"Many Rivers To Cross"
Mercury • 314522915-2

New Kids On The Block
"Face The Music" (album)
Sony Music • ck 52969

Elton John
"Duets" (album)
MCA • 10926

The Bodyguard (Soundtrack)
Whitney Houston/Various Artists
Arista • 18699-2

Al Jarreau
"Heaven And Earth" (album)
Reprise • 9 26849-2

Peabo Bryson
"Can You Stop The Rain" (album)
Columbia • ck 46823

The O'Jays
"Emotionally Yours" (album)
Phily International • 7-93390-2

Shanice
"Inner Child" (album)
Motown • 3746363192

Patti LaBelle
"Be Yourself" (album)
MCA • MCAD-6292

Aretha Franklin
"Through The Storm" (album)
Arista • AL- 8572

WEB SITE CONTENT

There are some things that words alone cannot explain, so I have included audio and video examples on the companion Web site. You can find these files and more at www.courseptr.com/downloads.

CHAPTER 2

General Knowledge Quiz . . . . ws_02-01.pdf

CHAPTER 3

Microsoft Word Business Card Template . . . . ws_03-01.doc

Pagemaker Business Card Template . . . . ws_03-02.pm65

Illustrator Business Card Template . . . . ws_03-03.ai

Promotional Tools Budget . . . . ws_03-04.xls

CHAPTER 8

Feedback . . . . ws_08.01.mp3

Headphone Bleed . . . . ws_08.02.mp3

Different Types of Reverb . . . . ws_08-03.mp3

Different Types of Digital Delay . . . . ws_08-04.mp3

CHAPTER 9

Examples of Untuned and
Digitally Tuned Vocals . . . . ws_09.01.mp3

The Vocal Cords in Action . . . . ws_09.02.mp4

Choosing The Right Key
(The National Anthem) . . . . ws_09.03.mp3

CHAPTER 10

Glossary

A

A Cappella. A vocal performance without instrumental accompaniment.

A&R (Artist and Repertoire). The division of a record label that is responsible for scouting and developing talent. The A&R department is the liaison between the recording artist and the record company. Part of the duties of this department include finding songwriters and record producers for the recording artist as well as scheduling recording sessions.

AFTRA (The American Federation of Television and Radio Artists). A performer's union that represents actors, radio and television announcers and newspersons, singers, and dancers in radio and television, commercials, and sound recordings.

Accompanist. A performer, such as a pianist, who plays an accompaniment.

Advertising Agency. A business that provides the service of producing advertisements for commercial products or services.

Aiff/Aif. Acronym for *Audio Interchange File Format*. An audio file format standard used for storing sound data on personal computers, which was originally developed for use on Apple computers.

Air. To broadcast on radio or television.

Airtime. The time during which something is being broadcast either on the radio or television.

Amplifier/Amp. An electronic device used to amplify an incoming audio signal from musical instruments or other sources, which is then coupled to loudspeakers for audible output.

Arbitration. The use of a neutral party to resolve a dispute.

Audition. A tryout by a singer to demonstrate performing skills.

Audition Reel/Audition Tape/Demo Reel/Demo DVD/Demo CD/Demo Tape. A recording of audio and/or video of your performance that was prepared for the specific purpose of submission to record companies, commercial production companies, etc., so that your talent can be evaluated.

B

Background Singer/Background Vocalist. A vocalist who backs up a featured vocalist or instrumentalist with harmonies, responses, and choruses on a recording.

Bar. Sections, typically of equal time value, into which a musical composition is divided.

Baffle/Gobo. A moveable shield that is placed around a microphone to keep out unwanted sounds.

Beaming. Transferring files between two devices by means of their infrared ports.

Biography/Bio. A written synopsis of someone's life, which is usually written by someone else.

Bleed. In recording, leakage occurring when sound emanating from one source (e.g., a headset, instrument, or amplifier) is picked up by a microphone placed to pick up sound from another source.

Blend. A balance of volume and timbre within a group of vocalists.

Bluetooth. A standard for the short-range wireless interconnection of cellular phones, computers, and other electronic devices.

Book (verb). (1) To schedule an appearance or make an appointment. (2) To engage a vocalist(s) and/or musician(s) for a performance. (3) To hire a studio or other facility for a recording or performance. (4) To reserve time.

C

Call Time. The time a performer is scheduled to arrive at a recording session.

Chart. A written arrangement or part for musical instruments or vocalists.

Circumaural. Headphone pads that go around your ears.

Cold. A quick, unrehearsed run-through of a performance.

Collective Bargaining. When an organized body of employees (a union) engages in the process of negotiating wages and other conditions of employment with an employer.

Commercial. An advertisement aired on television or radio.

Common Time. A rhythmic pattern in which there are four beats per bar and the beat unit is a quarter note. This pattern occurs often in classical music and is the norm in rock, jazz, hip-hop, R&B, country, and bluegrass.

Comp Track. Short for composite track. A final track made up of various parts or elements of other tracks.

Compressor. A signal-processing device used in recording and mixing to limit the range of dynamic responses from sound sources in order to present a more even, less erratic volume level.

Contingency Scale Payment. The royalty payable to non-royalty AFTRA artists whose performances are included on commercially released recordings. The amount of earnings paid is contingent upon the number of recordings sold.

Contractor/Session Leader/Contractor. The person who acts as the coordinator or leader of a recording session for a music producer or record company. Duties can include contacting the singers, conducting singers, rehearsal, minor rearranging of vocal parts, or any other similar supervisory duties.

Control Room. A room separated from a studio area that contains the mixing console and recording equipment and in which the engineer or producer oversees the recording of a performance.

Cue Mix/Headphone Mix/Cue Mix. In a recording studio, a cue mix is the headphone link between musicians and vocalists that allows each individual to hear his or her own performance in context with those of other musicians, vocalists, and previously recorded tracks.

D–F

Digital Audio Workstation (DAW). A system consisting of three elements: a computer, an interface, and software that is able to record, manipulate, and play back digital audio.

Digital Delay. A digital signal-processing device used in recording and mixing to electronically add or adjust the delay of an audio signal to give the perception of "slap echo" or doubling.

Discography. A comprehensive list of the recordings made by a particular performer.

Domain Name. A custom identifier for a Web site; a custom Web address. When you buy a new car, the Department of Motor Vehicles assigns it a license number. You can, however, acquire a custom license made for your car within the limits of what phrases are available. Also, there are limitations regarding the number and type of characters that can be used. Similarly, when you set up a Web site with a hosting company, the Web site is assigned an IP address (Internet Protocol address), which is usually a set of numbers. If you want to have a more memorable address for your Web site, you can get a domain name that can be used in place of the IP address when people want to access your Web site. Also, just like the custom license plates, there are similar limitations with regards to domain name phrase availability and the amount and type of characters used.

Doubling. Recording an additional track electronically or mechanically, duplicating the same material as recorded on the original track.

8 by 10. 8-inch by 10-inch sized promotional photos are often referred to in this way.

Fader/Slider. The control device on a mixer, recorder, or playback system by which sound levels are changed.

Feedback. An unwanted audio noise caused by the return of sound from headphones through the input source of the microphone.

Flat. To play an instrument or sing below the proper or indicated pitch.

Flat Fee/Buy Out. A one-time fee, usually paid up front, for the privilege of obtaining a license or the retention of professional services, as opposed to royalties, wages, or other forms of continuing compensation.

G–I

GB (Gigabyte). A way of measuring the data capacity of computing items such as hard drives, CDs, DVDs, computer memory, etc. A gigabyte is roughly equal to one billion bytes, with a byte being one unit of memory size.

Gig. A job, especially a booking for musicians.

Gold/Platinum. Part of a system enacted by the Recording Industry Association of America (RIAA) in 1958 to certify the sales of a sound recording. Gold status indicates the sale of 500,000 copies, while Platinum status indicates the sale of 1,000,000 copies. The RIAA is a trade group that represents the United States recording industry.

Headphone Amplifier. A device used to power and control the volume of headphones.

Headphones/Cans/Headset/Earphones. A binaural audio output device, usually fitted to the ears with a band passing over the head.

Hook/Chorus. The part of a song that is repeated after each verse, typically by more than one singer, and that gives it immediate appeal and makes it easy to remember. The term *hook* also has another, more metaphoric connotation: a phrase that was meant to catch the ear of the listener.

Hot/Live. On.

I-9. A federal form used by employers to determine an employee's citizenship and legal eligibility to work in this country.

In Tune. To sing the proper or indicated pitch.

Industrial. Recording projects that are usually produced for large corporations or trade associations to introduce new products and sales promotions, etc.

Infrared. A short-range wireless data transfer system. PDAs, laptop computers, and a host of other devices include infrared ports that enable them to communicate via a light beam.

Isolation Booth/Iso Booth/Vocal Booth. A smaller room built inside of a studio, usually constructed with nonreflective walls that eliminate potential reverberations.

J–L

Jingles. Short, catchy songs that are recorded and broadcast in TV or radio commercials.

JPEG/JPG. Acronym for Joint Photographic Experts Group; pronounced "jay-peg." JPEG is a type of digital image file used mostly on the Internet.

Karaoke Tracks. Prerecorded backing tracks of popular songs that people can sing to.

Key. The interrelationship between tones based on the seven tones of a major or minor scale and centered around a fundamental tone, usually called the tonic.

Labor Union. An organized association of workers, often in a trade or profession, formed to protect and further the rights and interests of its members.

Lead Sheet. Musical notation containing a song's melody line, together with lyrics and chord symbols, but not fully orchestrated (see Figure 9.1).

Lead Vocal/Lead Vocalist/Lead Singer. To be the featured singer.

Logo. A symbol or other small design used by an organization or person to identify its products or services.

Lyric Sheet. A sheet that contains the words to a song.

M–O

MB (Megabyte). A way of measuring the data capacity of computing items such as hard drives, CDs, DVDs, computer memory, etc. A megabyte is roughly equal to one million bytes, with a byte being one unit of memory size.

Member Report. A union member fills out this report as a record of what went on during the job. It is also the union's resource for filing claims in case the payment to the member is incorrect. In AFTRA, member reports are used for commercials, non-broadcast, sound recording, and interactive jobs. In SAG, they are used for off-camera singing jobs.

Metronome. A device used by musicians that marks time at a selected rate by emitting a regular tick.

Mic (verb). To strategically place a microphone close to the origin of a sound (i.e., a voice or instrument) in order to most faithfully capture, reproduce, transmit, or record the sound.

Microphone/Mic. A device that converts sound waves into an electrical signal. Microphones are used in many applications such as telephones, tape recorders, hearing aids, motion picture production, live and recorded audio engineering, radio and television broadcasting, and in computers for recording voice and numerous other computer applications.

Microphone Patterns. The shape of the physical space in which a microphone can detect, or "hear," sounds. Most microphones have one of three common listening patterns:

Omni. All around the mic, in a circle-shaped listening pattern.

Cardioid. A heart-shaped listening pattern.

Figure Eight. A bidirectional listening pattern.

Mix. To combine and blend two or more separately recorded tracks into one or two equalized tracks.

Mixer/Board/Mixing Console. An electronic device used by recording engineers to combine several audio signals onto one or more tracks on a segment of a computer hard drive (or a magnetic tape).

mp3. *MPEG-1 Audio Layer 3* is a digital audio encoding and compression format designed to reduce the amount of data needed to represent audio.

Multi-tracking. Recording additional tracks electronically or mechanically, containing the same material as recorded on the original track.

Musicianship. The art of being skilled in music.

MusicPro. A company that offers insurance coverage for instruments and equipment, studio liability, tour liability, travel accident, health insurance, life insurance, and long-term care.

Networking. The process of meeting people who might be an integral part of your career.

Number Chart System. A shorthand method of writing musical arrangements, originally developed by Nashville studio musicians. The method involves reducing a chord chart to equivalent numerical expressions

Octave. A tone that is eight full tones above or below another given tone.

Offset Printing. A process in which the inked image is transferred (or "offset") from a plate first to a rubber blanket and then to the printing surface.

Overdubbing. The process of recording new vocals, instrumental parts, or sound effects on additional tracks in synchronization with previously recorded tracks.

Overscale. When a vocalist receives more than minimum union scale payment for work on a project.

P–R

Pan. To direct a sound signal from left to right, right to left, or to the center of a stereo image.

PDA. Personal digital assistants are handheld devices that are designed to act as personal organizers, although some can also receive and send e-mail, view Web sites, act as cellular phones, run video games, and much more.

Preamp/Preamplifier. An electronic device commonly used to amplify microphones, electronic instruments, and other electronic devices.

Producer. A person or an organization that creates or caused to be created a product for sale; that organizes, guides, and shapes a product from conception to actuality.

Promotion. The planning and execution of any and all activities necessary to sell your products or services.

Proximity Effect. An exaggerated increase in low-frequency response occurring when the sound source is near the microphone. A loss in bass response is experienced as the microphone is moved away.

Punch In. The act of putting a recording device into record mode in order to insert or overdub new or additional material.

Punch Out. The act of taking a recording device out of record mode.

Recording Engineer. One who is trained or professionally engaged in capturing, maintaining, manipulating, and mixing audio performances.

Reference Vocal. A vocal frequently used solely for demonstration.

Release Date. The date that something (e.g., a book, CD, magazine, etc.) is made available, distributed, or sold to the public.

Residual/Reuse Fee/Replay Fee. An additional payment due a performer each time his work (on a television show or commercial, etc.) is rebroadcast.

Reverb. Electronic devices used in recording, playback, and mixing to simulate natural reverb effects. In the DAW's realm, there are digital versions of these devices called plug-ins.

Riff. A short melodic phrase, usually improvised by an instrumentalist or vocalist.

Royalty Artist. A person who is compensated for his or her services as a recording artist by royalties paid on each unit (records, CDs, cassettes, etc.) manufactured, distributed, and/or sold.

S

SAG (The Screen Actors' Guild). A labor union that represents actors in film, television, industrials, commercials, and music videos.

Scale. Minimum wage rate(s) or forms of compensation for union employees and contractors as specified in union agreements for specific types of employees or specific types of work.

Session/Recording Session. A period of time scheduled for recording music or vocals.

Sharp. Playing an instrument or singing above the proper or indicated pitch.

Side. Each track recorded (counting each overdub, multi-track, etc. as an additional side). This term is used mostly when dealing with union record (or as they say, phonograph) projects.

Signatory/Signator. A company or entity that has signed a contract or letter of agreement with the union, agreeing to terms regarding wages and working conditions for the members of that union.

Snippet. An abbreviated version of an audio file (song) or video.

Studio. A specially designed, constructed, and equipped room or facility used for audio recording.

Supra-aural. The headphone pads rest on your ears

T

Taft–Hartley. A federal law that permits a non-union performer to work for a union signatory, under a union contract, for a period of 30 days. After that time, the performer must join the union in order to accept any additional union work.

Take. A version of a recorded performance.

Talkback. A communication device that links performers in the studio with a producer or engineer in the control room and gives the engineer or producer the ability to talk to the performers from the control room.

TEIGIT (The Entertainment Industry Group Insurance Trust). TEIGIT was founded in 1965 in an effort to provide affordable insurance for actors and musicians by devising a system that allows members of guilds to join together to get group rates.

Thermograph Printing. Also called thermography or raised-ink lettering. This printing process creates a raised image on things like business cards, letterhead, or envelopes.

TIFF/TIF. Acronym for *Tagged Image File Format*; one of the most widely supported file formats for storing digital images on personal computers.

Timbre. The distinguishing character or quality of a musical sound or voice.

Track. A discrete or distinguishable strip or path along the length of a magnetic tape (or a segment of a computer hard drive) on which data or sound can be recorded and played back separately from the other tracks on the tape (or computer hard drive).

Track Sheet. A form used by recording engineers, mixers, and producers to plan, make note of, and identify which tracks on a magnetic tape (or a segment of a computer hard drive) are allocated or assigned to various instruments or voices.

Trade Organization. An association of people engaged in a particular area of business organized for a specific purpose.

Trade Show. A large gathering of manufacturers of a particular classification of products.

Transpose. Playing a song in a key different from the original key.

U–W

Vibrato. A pulsating effect produced in a vocal tone by barely perceptible, minute, and rapid variations in pitch.

W-4. A federal tax form used by an employer to determine the amount of deductions that should be taken from an employee's paycheck.

Wav/Wave. Short for Waveform audio format. An audio file format standard used for storing sound data on personal computers, originally developed for use on PCs.

Windscreen/Pop Filter. Any device or porous material placed in front of or over a microphone to control the relative intensity of sound waves.

Index

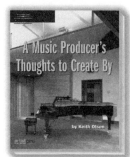

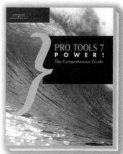